SHOPPING FOR A YANKEE SWAP

JULIA KENT

eBook ISBN: 9781950172597

Print ISBN: 9781950172603

Cover designer: Yocla Designs

Editor: Elisa Reed

SHOPPING FOR A YANKEE SWAP

Christmas is nostalgia heaven for my family. (Unless you count the Christmas tree fire, which we won't...)

Mom owns more holiday decorations than twelve area malls combined. Dad prides himself on hand chopping the best live tree, while my older sister has perfected peppermint cookies to the point of unparalleled bliss, and my younger sister has memorized every Christmas carol with her fingers for a piano bash that goes on and on.

And *on*.

But this year, Christmas is different.

This year, the McCormick men are joining the Yankee Swap.

You know how it works, right? Bring the craziest gift you can possibly find, pick a number, open the presents in order, and play "steal the gift" until person number one gets the last chance to snatch victory from the jaws of defeat.

My husband, Declan, is on a mission to win. He's so sure he can find the absolutely, positively, unreservedly weirdest gift, and he's willing to go to any extreme to find it.

Any extreme.

That's right: He's going thrift store shopping with my mother. The billionaire and the queen of frugal are on a *quest*.

Only one can win.

And on Christmas evening, after we're stuffed silly, sung out, and the kids fall asleep, the adults will break out the bizarre presents and the alcohol. It'll be showtime.

Because there ain't no competition like a McCormick competition.

But the Jacoby family has a trick or ten up its sleeves, too.

Note: Short portions of this novel appeared in Australia: A Romance Anthology *(which raised more than $100,000 USD for the wildfires there) and in* Filthy 2*, an audiobook-only anthology. These sections have been edited, new portions have been added, and this book is now an original, full novel with so much more in it.*

1

Shannon

"You're killing me, Shannon," Declan says over the Facetime video chat we're having. He's in Australia, on a quick layover for some meetings with a resort chain that might carry our coffee. A few years ago, as a wedding present, Declan bought me Grind It Fresh!, a small coffee chain with the best coffee I'd ever tasted. Some men would buy their new wife a necklace, or a fancy bike, or a special memento.

Mine went a little overboard.

We co-own and co-manage the chain of coffee shops. I handle on-the-ground issues at our headquarters here in Boston. He's the road warrior. His trip to Indonesia to negotiate Fair Trade coffee deals has been a big success, but he's been gone for three weeks.

Three entire weeks.

Three weeks of no sex. Three weeks of no kisses. Three weeks of no one to turn to for a silent hug, a quick smile, a simple vent. Yes, we have phones and texts and video chats, but it's no replacement for your lover's hot breath on the back of your neck as he initiates what you've been wanting, too.

The red garters had to come out, even if all we can do is have virtual sex.

Given that he just missed Thanksgiving yesterday, and Christmas is coming soon, I might need to pull out my sexy elf costume for old time's sake.

"I'm killing you? How about I kill you with my thighs wrapped around your face?" I tease.

His hand goes to his belt, pants unbuttoned, fly unzipped, one part of his body *very* much alive. Declan has eyes the color of heathered emeralds, framed by a strong face with broad cheekbones, and thick, dark hair. He stands tall, his shoulders straight, with a confidence that comes naturally. Unruffled and unraveled before me, half naked and breathing with a rough edge that speaks to desperation, I watch him on screen, a small smile curving my lips.

In public, he's an impenetrable wall, a steel fortress, an airtight container of business might and financial savvy.

In private, he's *mine*.

And I'm the one who brings him to the point of panting, holding his erection in one fist, staring at the red garters that made him lose his mind a few years ago, and imagining plunging into *me*.

"Those damn garters. I'm imagining you in my office that day. Remember? On my desk?"

"How could I forget?"

The sound of his ragged breath makes me feel less silly. Since we had our baby two years ago, Declan's traveled significantly less, but running a fast-growing coffee brand doesn't lend itself to a lot of time at home. We manage. Declan and Ellie have a standing date for Facetime video calls, and he reads her bedtime stories every night, even if it means he does it with his morning coffee from halfway around the globe.

We chat constantly, dealing with business issues, weaving in personal-life conversations.

But no video camera, no internet connection, no unlimited data plan is a substitute for having my husband naked in bed with me.

None.

"Are we really doing this?" I giggle.

"Pretty sure I'm about done," he says, but I can see he is definitely not. It's dark here, late at night, which means it's afternoon there.

I guess I'm having a nooner at midnight.

I move my face as close as possible to the camera.

"Shannon, what are you doing?"

"Put it right by your camera," I order him.

One eyebrow goes high. "Put... what?"

"You know."

I can't see anything, because my mouth is right up against my video lens, but I sure can hear.

"What the hell are you–oh, no. No. *No*." That last *no* sounds like a growl.

"What? It's the closest I can get–I'm simulating!"

"First of all, that's not even *close* to what your mouth feels like. Second of all, you're asking me to put my junk on a glass screen and... what? Move it up and down?"

"You can't exactly poke it at the screen and pretend it's a wet hole."

"This thing is so hard, it might *make* a hole."

"Declan!" My cry of outraged hilarity makes me stop, mid-sound.

I realize I've gone and done it.

You know that movie, *A Quiet Place?* The one where monsters track humans by sound and kill them if they even snap a twig?

That's one big metaphor for parenting a small child, let me tell you.

"Mama? MAMAMAMAMAMAMAMAMAMAMA," Ellie cries out from her bedroom next to ours.

"NO!" Declan grunts, then lets out an aggrieved sigh. "Damn it."

"No sex," I say with a sigh.

"Makes me feel like I'm right back home."

I wince. He's not wrong. But it hurts, anyhow.

Toddlers are the OG cockblockers.

Yanking the sash of my chiffon robe together as I stand, I tie it off, looking back at the screen to find Declan looping his belt. The robe is last year's Christmas present from my husband, one he selected just for this purpose.

"I'm sorry."

"Me, too." He looks at his crotch. The thick outline of his erection is obvious, even on video.

"MAMAMAMAMAMA! I want up! I want up!"

I close my eyes, trying to shut out the spike of the immediate reaction her cries generate in me. Shifting roles from sex kitten to mother isn't second nature, so I feel weirdly exposed as I look down at my breasts, uncovered for Declan's viewing. These same breasts feed my child.

How they're being used by others controls how I feel about them.

I grab the tablet, not ready to let go of my only connection to my husband.

Can you tell we've done too many of these FaceTime calls? We're the Facetime Family.

My throat aches a bit at the thought, stinging with emotion.

And speaking of Christmas, he needs to get home soon. Our third Christmas with Ellie needs to be extra special; her first Christmas, my parents' house caught on fire during the festivities, so that one doesn't really count.

Our cat, Chuckles, still has half his tail fur burnt off.

Last year we all sat around Mom and Dad's still-under-renovation living room and tried not to tempt fate. The Yankee Swap was a half-hearted, Jacoby-only event.

None of the usual suspects came to the celebration.

This year is different. More than needing to reclaim good memories, we have been presented with a challenge from my mother.

The great Jacoby Yankee Swap will resume this year, and I'm determined that my husband will join in.

"Up! Uppy!" Ellie calls again, only this time, her tone is less frantic, her language devolving into baby talk. I have a chance to take a true, deep breath and feel my inner arms brush against my lower ribs as I move, the tablet pressing into my side.

"If we had a live-in nanny, you wouldn't need to do this," says a voice from under my left arm.

I tap the back of the tablet's case and say loudly, "If we had a live-in nanny, you'd get less sex, because I can't make love with you when someone else is here."

Walking into Ellie's room, I find her red faced, eyes teary and wide. Her little arms reach for my neck and soon, she's clinging to me, tiny ribs wracked with aftershocks from crying.

"*Shhhhhhh*," I say as I sway-walk back to my bedroom and hold the tablet screen toward her. Declan stares back at us, the image cutting him off at the waist on the display screen.

"Hi, Ellie!" he coos, instantly in Awesome Dad mode, making me smile. My father and Declan are about as different as two men can be, but in this–loving and parenting their child–they are one and the same.

"Dah-dee!" Ellie squeals, touching the screen. "Whatcha doon?"

"I am in Australia!"

"Uh-stray-la?"

"Yes! Good! I'll be home in two days."

"I want Daddy home. I want swings whichoo."

"Swings! Of course. How many pushes?"

"All da pushes!"

A wistful look takes over his face. I know that look. It's the expression of a man who would rather be here than where he actually is. Ambition is in his DNA, but loving his daughter takes precedence.

"All the pushes, sweetie," he says as Ellie kisses the glass screen.

"I want milk, Mama," she says. "Chocka milk."

"How about water?" I offer. Sexytime is over. Parenting mode engaged. "Water and some cantaloupe."

"Catnayope!" she crows, toddling off to the kitchen in her footed sleeper. As she leaves, Chuckles pokes his head into the room. He spots Declan, and I swear the cat smiles.

"Want me to put Chuckles on? He can kiss the screen for you."

"That's the only pussy I'm getting, apparently," Declan mutters.

I stick my tongue out at him. He doesn't laugh.

A huff, then a long sigh comes from the screen as he runs his hand through his hair, conflicted eyes growing larger on the screen as he leans in and says, "I'm not sure I want this anymore."

"Want what?"

"This." He motions with his hands, as if gesturing to the whole wide world. "All the travel."

"You can build a coffee empire without it."

"No, Shannon. I can't."

"You can come home and focus on other aspects of the business. Or you could retire."

"Retire? I'm not that old!"

"Retirement isn't just for old people."

"But I love what I do. I just hate being away from you and Ellie."

"You're the boss. Change it."

A wry grin spreads across his face. "You're right."

"I am?"

"I've been gone from you for too long. I miss you."

"I know. Three weeks without sex is a long time."

"No–not the sex. I miss *you*. I miss my friend. I miss hearing you laugh. Your breath on my face. Your cold feet against my calves. How you smell in bed. Moving furniture around because you want to make a play area in the living room for Ellie. Going to vintage antique shops and buying weird sculptures."

"Since when do you miss going to thrift shops with me? And they're not weird!" I bring the tablet into the kitchen with me, where I find Ellie on the floor, the tub of pre-cut cantaloupe in her lap, each little fist clutching an orange chunk.

The fridge door is wide open, casting a sci-fi glow over her.

"You bought a gnome drinking coffee out of a toilet, Shannon."

"For this year's Yankee Swap!"

"The gnome had a frog on a leash."

"It's supposed to be funny!"

"And when you press the button, it sounds like an octopus being choked to death."

"Your point is...?"

He makes a grunting sound worthy of Geralt of Rivia.

"Fine," I inform him as Ellie thrusts her sticky fingers into the venting grate under the fridge. "Next time we go to a thrift shop, you get to find something better."

"I'll just send Dave."

"You cannot send your executive assistant to find a Yankee Swap present!"

"Of course, I can."

The silence is what makes me suspicious.

"Declan?"

Another grunt.

"You had Dave shop for you this year, didn't you?"

Another grunt.

Suppressing the impulse to sing the first line of "The Witcher" song and toss a coin his way, I turn the video camera on Ellie instead.

"Say hi to Daddy!"

"Hi, Daddy! You want some catnayope?" She smears a greyish, half-chewed piece on the glass where Declan's mouth is.

"Mmmmmm," he pretends. "Yum!"

Talking with my husband for two minutes instead of monitoring her has led to a twenty-minute clean up.

"I knew it! Daddy yikes catnayope!"

"Nice sentences!" he says, grinning.

"She's been saying more complex phrases all week," I tell him.

His face falls. "She has? I missed it." Voice going gruff, he turns negative. "Damn."

"Dam!" Ellie repeats.

"Shit," he mutters.

"That doesn't help!" I say through gritted teeth.

"I mean, I like it!" Over-enunciating, he uses the time-tested technique every parent tries when they utter profanity in front of the human equivalent of a mynah bird.

"I yike it!" Ellie repeats.

Magic.

The man has magical powers. If I said the S-word, Ellie would repeat it *ad infinitum,* and always in the worst possible places. At the pediatrician, during story hour at the library, at the yarn shop Mom loves, where the woman who runs it looks like a church organist–you get the picture.

Declan does it? Crisis averted.

Chuckles pads up to the screen and starts licking Declan's face. When I try to pet him, I get a condescending sniff.

Dec laughs.

Chuckles runs off.

"I miss being home," Declan says. Squaring his shoulders, he nods to himself. "And it's entirely my fault."

"Your fault?"

"Which means it's completely under my control."

"Huh?"

"If something is a person's fault, there's a cause-effect relationship. You can't be held accountable for something you can't control, but I can control being away from my family."

"Yes, you can. You're the boss. The owner. The CEO. What you do with your time is completely your decision," I affirm.

"And I've been deciding to be away. It felt like it was inevitable, but it's not. Not if I say no."

"Say no to yourself?"

"Say no to the idea that in order to be successful, I have to do it like this." Eyes the color of an Irish hill meet mine. "I chose. I have the power."

"You always do."

"I'm a hypocrite."

"You are? How?"

"I lectured Andrew before the twins were born. Came down hard on him about putting work ahead of his growing family. What do they call that in psychological terms? Projection?"

"Since we've had Ellie, you've been a very hands-on father. I know you and Andrew worry about being like *your* father, but neither of you is anything like James."

His shoulders drop with relief. "I know. And I don't think Andrew will be like Dad, but I laid into him. We had that fight, and he came damn close to hitting me."

"I didn't hear about *that* part."

A rueful stretch of Declan's mouth makes it clear the incident had an emotional impact on him. For as much as I hate having him away from us so much, these Facetime sessions paradoxically tend to get him to open up to me more.

"He told me he wanted to run the gym chain he'd bought, *and* be CEO, *and* be a new father to the twins. Plus a husband to Amanda. I told him he was crazy, and he brushed me off. It got... tense."

"When was this?"

"At the end of Amanda's pregnancy."

"The twins are fifteen months old, Dec! You never told me."

"I know."

"If he almost hit you, sounds like it got more than just tense."

"We're fine now. But I'm thinking back on it and realizing *I'm* the one traveling all over the place and *he's* back there in Boston, winding down his responsibilities at Anterdec."

Andrew quit his role as CEO of their family company last May, on Mother's Day.

As we all gathered at their mother's grave.

"Amanda said it'll take him nearly two years to really leave."

"She's right. You don't just give two weeks' notice when you're the CEO of a Fortune 500 company. And Dad's doing everything he can to maintain control, which isn't helping."

"He's also frozen Andrew out. Nothing like the silent treatment to make everything better."

A long, pained sigh comes out of Declan. "Never underestimate the stubborn narcissism of the founder of a large institution."

"This isn't just founder's syndrome, though, Declan. James is acting like Andrew doesn't exist," I say, disgust and pain echoing back from my own voice.

"I know. It's immature and ridiculous, which is exactly what I would expect from Dad."

"I'm so glad you're nothing like him."

"Me, too." He groans. "Except here I am, gone for three weeks on yet another business trip. It's exactly what the 1990s were like, growing up with him."

"You are not him!"

"And I don't want to lose these years with you. With Ellie. With our other children."

"Other children?" A tingle forms in my belly.

"Shannon, I–" A distinct buzz cuts him off, the sound of a notification coming in. "Damn it."

"JAM IT!" pipes up a little voice behind me. I turn and look down.

Ellie's using a potholder to smoosh cantaloupe pieces into the planks of the hardwood floor.

"I have to go. Some sort of problem with air travel out of Australia."

"Oh, no!"

Ellie looks at me, eyes wide, reading my emotions.

"It's fine. I mean, it's not fine, of course. I'll be home in two days. No matter what."

"Good!"

"MAMA!" Ellie screeches, holding up a red finger. "I got a boo-boo!"

"Let Daddy kiss it," Declan says, and I hold her finger to the screen.

"Mwah!" kisses my billionaire husband, being as goofy and lovesick with his daughter as I've ever seen him.

"Dat better, Daddy!" She gives him a very sticky kiss.

I blow him one. You think I'm kissing that tablet screen now? Ewww.

"See you soon. I love you."

"I love you, too, Dec."

"And I mean it. I'm redefining how I build Grind It Fresh! There is a better way, and I'll find it."

"I know you will. You'll find your way home."

2

Shannon

Two Days Later

It's three a.m. and Ellie, who is cutting yet another molar, is finally asleep, her slumber like the steady sound of the ocean lapping at the shore. It's hypnotic, really, a sound I could listen to for the rest of my life and never tire of it. When awake, she's a whirling dervish, needing constant attention.

In slumber, she draws me in, too, a work of art to behold.

Dec texted me earlier to tell me he'd be home around five a.m. If I hold out, I can greet him at the door, but my long yawn as I move into our kitchen tells me that's not happening. Sleep is the valuable currency of parenthood at this stage of our lives.

I'm not spending it all on the hope he'll be home on time.

A brewed cup of chamomile helps me unwind. So, too, does the lovely new photo album my mother and father put together for us. Mom's been going through all our old family photos, and Dad took eighteen years of digital camera archives and printed the best shots. Between the two, they created cherished albums, custom made for me and my sisters.

Cameras, in my childhood, were pulled out for special occasions, and a photo of a group was carefully arranged. You had twenty-four takes on a roll of film, and processing was expensive. For my parents, who barely scraped by so Mom could stay home with Carol, Amy, and me, you didn't waste film.

I already have my baby book, the early '90s photos stamped on the back with York Photo, a mail-order service that kept the cost of developing film down. Mom and Dad never, ever used the photo huts or the place in the mall, where prices were higher.

But once they got their first digital camera in 2002 (a Black Friday deal Dad still talks about: the tent in front of the big-box electronics store, the record low temperature of eleven degrees, the glares as he got the last camera at $79), that was it. Photos were now stored on a drive, hard or flash or thumb, so all our memories were preserved–but not in front of us.

This present? This is pure gold.

The baby book beckons now, too, right under the new album on the end table in the living room.

Mom, pregnant with me, my older sister Carol in her arms. Dad, his ear against Mom's belly, and in the next shot with Carol on his shoulders. All four of us, me in utero, in front of our house, which would have been brand new to them.

Then.

Now it's paid off.

I turn the page to see newborn me, in my sister's arms, Mom hovering as little preschooler Carol holds my eight-pound form in her spindly arms, a big grin testimony to how excited she was to be a big sister. Mom and Dad, standing in front of the hospital, me in a car seat.

Close-ups of me in a crib. In Dad's arms. On Mom's shoulder.

I'm sure Carol's baby book is longer, better, more detailed. Our younger sister, Amy, never fails to complain bitterly that hers is nothing more than black and white photos from the Chuck E. Cheese booth, school pictures, and tear-filled screamfests from mall-Santa photo packages.

An exaggeration, but she has a point.

I take a sip of my tea and stare at the fireplace, a gas insert we added for warmth and fun last year.

Ellie is my first. She's my Carol.

The next child we have will be my equivalent. Declan's a middle child, too.

We've produced an eldest.

When is it time for a middle? We know we want more than two. Four makes me a little nervous.

Three feels just right now that we've had one.

As I page through the albums, I find Dad cutting wood, Mom planting a vegetable garden with a baby in a stroller next to her. Every photo is simple, all at local parks, the house, and occasionally in Buffalo, where some of Dad's extended family is from. No trips to Disney, no shots at the Eiffel Tower, no big vacations.

I see tents. Backyard staycations. Remodeling projects and homegrown fun.

So different from what Declan and I can give to our children. I married into money, but I come from a family where every dollar wasn't just earned.

It had to earn its keep, too.

A tug at my heart makes me choke up as I look at the newer pictures. My nephews being born (no crotch shots, so no worries). A few pictures of my ex-fiancé, Steve. Mom cut him out of almost every single one, so carefully, it's like a surgeon did it.

But he's in larger group photos, in the back, looking uncomfortable.

So is Carol's ex, Todd, my nephews' father.

Years of change roll out as I turn the pages, all passing like blinks.

"You're right," I whisper to Declan, though he's not here. "You're missing out." Tears fill my eyes, the sour tingle of emotion breaking through.

I couldn't tell him that on the Facetime chat. It felt cruel. Ever since Ellie was born, I've wanted more of him than I wanted before.

Strange, right? Because you'd think I'd desire less, given the addition of a child. That the wanting of my husband would recede a bit.

No. It's only intensified with time.

Not just to have him here to build a life with our child.

To build a world with me. Just us. Making decisions,

supporting each other, being intimate, sharing this journey. No one knows why we're here on this planet, but I do know this: I wouldn't spend this lifetime partnered with anyone else.

Declan is it. He's my soulmate, my reincarnated partner, my energy lifeline, my core. Whatever you call it, whatever you believe, he's how I figure out who I am.

My husband is a witness to my growth, and a catalyst, too.

Stifling a yawn as I wipe my tears, I realize the chamomile did the trick. My gaze rests on a photo of Dec and me, taken the first time Mom and Dad met him, the day he came to the apartment I shared with my sister, Amy. It was a one-bedroom walk-up above someone's garage, in a town about a half hour from our parents. Dad sat on a dead mouse Chuckles had caught, and Declan got a glimpse of Mom's crazy.

He didn't bat an eyelash.

Okay, maybe one or two. But he stayed anyhow.

Someone surreptitiously caught him on camera, in profile, chatting with Dad before the Great Dead Mouse-capade, Chuckles nosing up against Dec's shin. Chuckles hates everyone, but not my husband.

Cats *know*.

The polite smile on Declan's face makes me wonder what he and Dad were talking about as I got ready for that first date. Second date? We'd already gone out for a business dinner that, to this day, I swear was *not* a date.

But Declan does.

His argument: He brought me a corsage. We kissed. Therefore, it's a date.

My argument: Well, how can I have one when he's *that* romantic?

I yawn. The clock on the stove reads 3:47 a.m. Chuckles sniffs and climbs off the chair next to me with a liquid motion that makes me wish I could be a cat for a day. What does it feel like to have bones that are jelly when you need them that way?

As I wander into the bathroom to brush my teeth, I start the process, using my free hand to open a drawer. My diaphragm rests in its case. Knowing Declan, he'll climb into bed naked, ready for action.

I need to be ready, too.

A tug in my belly makes a dangerous thought race through my mind.

What if we start on the middle child now?

"Mo," I say to myself in the mirror, mouth full of toothpaste foam. "Mot mifout docking to Deccan."

I rinse. I laugh. I put the cold silicone circle inside me and smile.

But it's a strangely sad smile.

My bed feels so good, if cold and empty. A comfortable mattress is worth its weight in gold, but the warm body of a man in love with me is priceless.

Before my mind can race through all the things I have to do tomorrow, I'm out.

THE KISS IN MY DREAM HAS A TASTE, LIKE COFFEE AND mint, like strawberry and relief. As I roll over to wrap my arms around Declan's neck, I halt.

This isn't a dream.

"Dec?" I whisper, fuzzy and half out of it, his elbow pressing my hair against the pillow.

"Mmm," he says as he kisses me again. "I'm home."

His erection taps against my thigh like a door-to-door salesman selling dildos.

"I can tell." A rush of heat pumps through me, his closeness a thrill. After three weeks of distance, this is almost too much, more than I could hope for.

He's home.

He's here.

And we're both so, *so* horny.

"How about a quickie?"

"It's always a quickie with Ellie around," I hiss as he pulls my panties down, in me before I can finish blinking, his mouth on my neck, tongue flicking the spot under my ear that drives me crazy. My legs are around his naked waist, the man completely bare, his ass familiar yet strangely new. I reach around him and squeeze as he thrusts long, slow, dangerous strokes into me.

"This is the best welcome I could possibly have," he murmurs in my ear as I make a sound of agreement.

"When did you get home?" I ask. The words turn into a gasp as I arch my hips toward him, the full sensation closing an open need in me.

"Thirty seconds ago."

"Took you that long to get naked? Slacker."

He laughs, the movement pressing his pelvis into me, my walls clenching tight in response. The amused rumble in him turns into a low groan, the kind that makes me wetter and hotter, my hands on the hem of my nightgown, pulling it up.

Until I realize I buttoned it high.

I am completely naked, every inch of me from the neck down pressed against nude Declan, but my face is covered by the nightgown.

"Is this some role-play thing you've been hiding from me, Shannon? Because you don't have to cover your face."

"Ghosting is a new kink I forgot to mention," I mumble, cotton in my mouth, as he laughs and tightens his thighs, moving his knees so he has his hands free to undo the button holding me hostage.

"I thought ghosting was when you disappear on someone."

"My mouth disappeared."

"I would never, ever want your mouth to go away, Shannon. Never ever. Your amazing mouth."

"Then help me get unstuck," I mutter, the cloth in the way.

"Kissing you through cotton isn't nearly as good as this," he murmurs as the nightgown pulls my long hair up over my head. His mouth is on my jawline, tongue dancing against mine as he resumes his rhythm.

After so many weeks without sex, our climaxes are quick, hard, simultaneous, and almost perfunctory. The emotion is there, but the physical need overrides sentimentality.

Plus, we have a small child. Get your orgasms in while you can. There's never a guarantee of round two, and sometimes even round one is called on account of...

Toddler.

I curl up in the crook of his arm and hear his heart go from a steady gallop to a simple beat, until he sits up, crawls out of bed, and paws through a small bag.

"What are you doing?"

"Getting your present."

"Now?"

In his hand, he holds a brown, crinkly pack of–

"TIM TAMS!" I gasp as my stomach lets out a gurgle so loud, you'd think an alien was about to pop out of it.

Declan shakes his head as I open the box. "Sorry they're crushed."

"Crushed, intact, they all taste the same!"

"You can buy them here in the U.S., Shannon. Dave can get them for you anytime."

"They don't taste the same."

"But you just said–"

I shove a cookie in his mouth.

We crawl back under the covers, both of us listening for Ellie.

"I want another one," Declan says suddenly.

I hand him a cookie.

"No–not that. Those are for you."

"Oh. Good. Because I wasn't going to be stingy, but..."

"I want another child, not another Tim Tam."

"Of course. We've talked about having more." I shake the container, sad to discover I really am eating the last one.

"I mean, I'm ready to start. Now."

"*Now?* Don't you need a little time for your refractory period to pass?"

"Not right this moment. But... I think it's time for us to stop using birth control. Ellie is two and a half. If we're lucky, the new baby will be a little more than three years younger. That seems reasonable."

I stroke his cheek. "It doesn't have to be reasonable."

"It doesn't?"

"You don't have to make a case, Declan. No flowcharts or PowerPoint decks required. You can appeal to me with emotion. I can stop using my diaphragm whenever we want."

"I want this," he says, voice low and hoarse. "I want us. I want you. And I want my family. *Our* family. The one we build together."

"I do, too."

He kisses me.

"*And* I want a house," I add. Hey, why not up the ante? If I have to rent out my entire body to a new human being with no lease, no payments, and the end result involves damage no security deposit could possibly cover, I want something out of the bargain.

"A house?"

"Yes."

"You don't like the condo?"

The bedroom door nudges open a few inches, making me realize that in Declan's rush to make love, he didn't close it. Ellie's at the point where she can climb out of her crib. Eek.

Since becoming a mother, I've found myself more modest. Less impulsive about sex. Not that I don't want it–I certainly do–but it's taken on a mystique. A holiness. A sense of reverence.

We used sex to make a human being out of love, lust, an egg, and a sperm.

Something so powerful *should* be taken seriously.

As I'm about to answer Declan's question, Chuckles leaps up onto the long bench at the end of our bed and settles in, mouth turning down, little fangs poking out as he closes his eyes and sighs.

"I want a garden," I start to explain.

"A garden?"

"You know–tomatoes and cucumbers and carrots and–"

"I know what a garden is. Why?"

"And goats."

"You want goats?"

"Chickens, too. Maybe ducks?"

"*Ducks?*"

"Their eggs are really good." I'm not even going to *mention* the llama.

"Where are we going to keep all these animals?"

"In the barn. On our land."

"You want to move out of the city and have a farm?" I play with the hair on his chest as his ribs rumble with a deep laugh, his fingers combing my mussed hair, our shared look one of affection and dreams.

"How about we start with a house and a dog and a garden?"

At the word *dog*, Chuckles lifts his chin off his paws and glares at me.

"*You* say dog next time," I whisper to Dec, breath against his chest. "He'll take it better from you. Right now, I'm pretty sure he's plotting how to steal my breath while I sleep."

"How about we start with the baby part and move on to the house after."

"You can't multitask?"

He laughs. "I see how this negotiation is going."

"Promise me we'll have a house before the next baby is born."

"I promise. Where do you want to move?"

"Wherever you are."

"Well, that's easy. I'll always be with you." He stiffens. "You don't want to move to Mendon, do you? Near your parents?"

"Not *that* far outside of Boston."

"Then where?" Before he finishes the words, he groans. "You want to move to Weston, don't you? Near my brother and Amanda."

"She *is* my best friend." I frown and look at him. "Wait a minute. This whole having-another-baby thing. Is this inspired by Andrew having twins? You want to catch up to your brother?"

He bristles at the words *catch up*. "No!"

"You two are so competitive."

"We are," he admits.

"I'll bet *he* brings Amanda *two* containers of Tim Tams whenever he comes home from a trip."

"You're not going to let this go, are you?"

I reach under the sheet and grab something else. "Nope." Signs of life appear. "Hmmm. You seem to be recovering nicely."

He yawns. "My jet lag has jet lag."

"*This* has no lag."

"You have to do all the work if you want another round."

I climb on top of him, straddling, easing him in with a comfortable stretch that makes us both groan with pleasure.

I kiss him, then pull back, hair in his face, his eyes shining in the early dawn light.

"Just like pregnancy. I do *alllll* the work," I tease.

"I would have a baby for you if I could."

"This one will be born in a hospital," I say firmly. "Not an elevator."

"Ellie's birth was a freak accident."

"Emphasis on *freak*."

"So was meeting you," he says as he nudges his hips up.

"I was just doing my job, evaluating the cleanliness of that men's room in your bagel shop!"

"This is not the kind of dirty talk I was imagining we'd do in bed when I got home, Shannon."

"Then find something else for my mouth to do."

The kiss that answers me is lush and roaming, a long, slow, wet ramble through the layers of me he can feel but can't name. When you've been with someone for enough years, you choreograph how you touch them. You don't realize it, but it's there, a series of patterns that fall into place without conscious thought.

The waist touch. The shoulder stroke. The love pat on the ass. The arm around shoulders or waist. Hand in hand or fingers threaded? Head on a shoulder or tucked into a chest? Chin on her head or her ponytail resting against your collarbone?

Palm on your knee while you drive? An arm under an elbow for support on outdoor deck stairs? A hand up out of a recliner while she's pregnant? A hand down on stairs to give him extra help?

And then there are the intimate connections, the endless variations of kisses and touches, of bare flesh against flesh, of tongues between legs and mouths of velvet. The push and pull, the up and down, the side to side and back to front. The heady insolence of all the ways you can use your body to love another person with all your heart, heat, and humanity.

Humor, too.

By the time Declan's finished kissing me, our second round of lovemaking well underway, I hear a little voice in the next room, babbling away like Ellie does.

See? Round two is never, ever a given.

Soon, she'll call out for Mama and when Daddy comes to pick her up instead, she'll shriek with laughter, arms extended for a hug she has come to rely on.

She knows he's there for her.

And that's really all anyone can do for anyone else, right?

Be there.

Because presence *matters*.

3

Declan

Dear Shannon,

Did you mean it?

I know you did, so that question is rhetorical.

Last night, after I came home from three straight weeks of travel to curl up against you, naked and hungry and one big ball of need, you were there.

The taste of your kiss, how your lips parted and your tongue met mine, the way you embraced me as I crawled into our bed, your legs parting so I could truly come home, made me feel like the richest man in the world.

Money doesn't make me wealthy.

You do.

Your love gave me a life. Your love (and gorgeous body) gave me a daughter. Your love saved me from a life where I only got to be one version of who I am. It's not a bad version, the driven CEO, the ruthless deal-maker who always–always–wins.

But that's only one part of me.

The rest of me deserves a shot at a life, too. The rest of me should have a chance to win in different ways.

And that's where you come in.

(Or, should I say, where I come in you.) Heh.

Thank you. You didn't have to love me, but you did. You do.

And I know you always will.

Love,

D

p.s. Next time I come home from a business trip, wear the red garters to bed.

p.p.s. Assuming you meant it, I'm at your service. Time to give Ellie a sibling.

I slide the handwritten note into an envelope embossed with my initials, and don't bother licking and sealing the envelope. Propping it on her pillow, I retreat, grinning as I close the door.

The apartment is quiet. A little *too* quiet. Ellie's already off with our nanny, Mia, and Shannon's at the office. When I'm home, I'm accustomed to more activity, with a toddler whose language is advanced enough to make me wonder what the teen years will be like and a wife who processes the world externally.

Verbally.

Constantly.

Don't get me wrong: She's nothing like her mother. Well, most of the time.

But when it comes to the verbal processing, the apple didn't fall far from the tree.

Speaking of which, a bowl full of shiny Honeycrisps catches my eye. I grab one, sinking my teeth into the sweet flesh just as my phone rings.

It's my assistant, Dave. I put him on speakerphone.

"Doublann Coffee is undercutting Grind It Fresh!'s bid by ten percent," he says bluntly, dispensing with the niceties in a manner I find deeply appealing. If I could have custom designed an executive assistant, I couldn't have done a better job than the guy who arbitrarily fell into the job.

He makes artisanal chocolate in his bathtub. He lives in a squatter's community in an old warehouse.

He's an *actual* Socialist.

And he's damn good at what he does for my company.

"Ten percent? Huh. No way they can make a profit on that level," I reply, trying to chew and swallow quickly so I can talk.

"I think they just want to undercut you. Drive you to the point of breaking."

I snort, nearly inhaling a chunk of apple. "Good luck with that."

"What's your approach?"

I wonder if my dad's longtime assistant, Grace, talked about deals with him like this. Was their relationship at this higher level? My brother, Andrew–who was heir to Anterdec, my father's company–has an executive assistant who speaks in questions, the end of every sentence a breathy lift that makes her sound young and stupid.

But is she?

"Dec? Hello?"

"Yes, I'm here."

"You're distracted."

"I'm..." He's right. But he can't know that.

"I'm thinking." I take another bite of apple and chew. It's sweet and juicy, like my wife.

My phone buzzes again. It's Andrew. I ignore it.

"Look, Peter Mullahy will be at the Neurological Institute fundraiser tonight," Dave begins.

"The what?" I mutter before swallowing.

"Do you ever look at your calendar?"

"No. Why would I? That's your job."

He doesn't even bother to sigh. "You have an event tonight. You and Shannon. Grind It Fresh! chose the Neuro Institute as a charitable cause, remember?"

"That's *tonight?*"

"Yes. And Mullahy from Coffee Central Holdings will be there. You can schmooze."

I let out the sound that zombies make when they see brains. "Perfect. I'll convince him we can perform better than Doublann."

"Of course, we can. Check out the PDF I sent you. I broke

down all of Doublann's weaknesses, complete with quick elevator speeches and talking points."

"Why aren't you running presidential campaigns, Dave?"

"Because the only person I would ever support in that role isn't running anymore."

"Right." I don't even want to know who that might be. "Drill down into Doublann's weaknesses. Work on holding the line on the bid. Convince CCH that we can give a higher quality result. Anything else?"

"Yeah. Your wife is ovulating."

"Excuse me?"

"You asked me to track her cycles last month." Dave clears his throat, a rarity. Is he nervous? The guy is never nervous.

Just like me.

"I did?"

"Yes, Declan, you did."

"Well. Okay. Thank you for, uh, doing that." Note to self: Give Dave an ovulation-tracking bonus.

"Act now."

"Excuse me?"

"Act *now*. The egg is only viable for twenty-four hours after ovulation. Sperm are good for at least two days. Your best shot is if the sperm are waiting for the egg when it arrives. You could miss your window if you don't act now."

"Do you know *everything*, Dave?"

"No. But I know *how* to know everything."

The call ends. My phone buzzes.

Driver is downstairs, ready for me.

I head to the office, where time escapes as I focus on nothing but choices. That's the true work of a CEO: making decisions.

Other people execute and implement.

I deliberate and approve.

My phone buzzes with a text, jerking me out of my tunnel vision. I look at the clock, wondering where four hours went.

The letter is lovely, Shannon types. *And I'm ready. I've been tracking my cycles.*

You went home? I reply.

Forgot my phone, she answers.

You're ovulating today, I type back.

An eye-popping emoji appears.

How did you know?

I'm tracking your cycles, too, I reply.

What? It's true. I am.

Okay. Fine. *Dave* technically is, but the brownie points still count in my column.

You are? OMG! I think that's the most romantic thing you've ever said to me, she answers, a full row of heart emojis following.

I can whisper plenty of romantic words in your ear, you know, I reply. *Especially when I'm between your legs.*

Save it for baby-making sex. No diaphragm. Meet you at home now? In your office? I'm on site at the shop down the street, she replies.

Bzzz

You have a four-hour meeting blocked out at the lender's office on State Street, Dave texts. *Car's waiting for you.*

My eyes bounce from his text to Shannon's.

How long is peak ovulation good for? Not standard ovulation. PEAK, I type out, catching myself just in time as I almost send this to Shannon.

I'm asking Dave.

I hit send.

Always optimizing, he says. *Today. Sperm need to be there when the egg drops.*

I calculate the time math. Damn it.

I have to go from the lender meeting straight to the fundraiser? I need an hour break, I double thumb, hoping there's an out here. The CCH deal is huge. Enormous. If we can start using their distribution system for our coffee chain, it'll allow scalability that substantially alters the course of our business.

And allows me to cut back on travel and be home more with my wife and child.

Or children.

No, he types back.

If, as Dave explained it, the sperm need to be there ahead of time, then this has to happen as soon as possible. That egg could drop at any moment. It could have already dropped.

I don't type that out, mulling it over. We could rush home and have a quickie immediately after the event, but what if it's too late?

No, Declan, I can't push back the lender meeting. You'll have to rush home after and fit it in, he says, reading my mind.

Fit it in.

Right.

We'll just have to find a way to fit it in.

4

Declan

HAVE YOU EVER HAD THE PLEASURE OF WATCHING your beautiful wife from afar at a formal event, the curve of her calves in high heels, a slinky, sequined dress sleek against her curves, long hair in an updo, her neck begging for kisses?

No?

Your loss.

I catch her eyes from across the room, her mouth stretched in a smile as she laughs at something Peter Mullahy is saying to her, the look on her face going from genuine pleasure to something damn close to carnal as our eyes lock.

Fingertips on Mullahy's forearm, she leans into him, whispers something, and then moves toward me.

Step by step, my desire for her grows.

Step by step, I lose myself in her gorgeous presence.

Step by step, her eyes turn cold, lips turning down, jaw tightening.

"You," she says loudly, the live music making it hard to hear, fingers curling into my biceps, the tuxedo thick enough to stop her from drawing blood. "You couldn't spare thirty minutes to come home and have a *quickie?*"

At the end of her sentence, the band stops playing, the words "...have a *quickie?*" hanging in the air.

Dave is standing on the other side of the raw bar, lips twitching as he holds back a smile.

A few titters, the hush of whispers, and then the band starts up again.

"Good to see you too, honey," I tell her, giving her made-up cheek the standard, respectable kiss a husband gives his wife at one of these gatherings.

My lips touch heated flesh.

"I can't believe I said that in front of two hundred people."

"Only ten or so of them heard it."

Dave walks over, hand wrapped around a highball glass. "More like twenty-five, given the radius around you." He nods at my wife, who gives him an eye roll and then, finally, a real smile. Shannon's in high heels and she towers over Dave, though the guy has a way of looking up at people that doesn't diminish his power.

"Thanks for tracking my cycle," she says to him. "Not that it did any good."

He goes still.

I leap into action.

"That dress officially makes you the most gorgeous woman in the room, Shannon," I say, meaning it.

"There's less butter in this shortbread tart than in your words, Declan," she responds, popping the sweet pastry in her mouth.

"I don't need to butter you up. You're warm and tasty and slick all on your own."

"Oh, God," Dave mutters, looking away. "Excuse me while I go stuff myself with Fair Trade, wild-caught salmon, goat cheese, and figs. Or a bucket of anchovies. Whatever it takes to get away from listening to *this*."

He departs. Shannon's grasp on my arm tightens.

"Seriously, you couldn't spare half an hour?"

"I couldn't."

"Really?"

Uh oh. Her voice is getting teary.

"Honey, I really couldn't. I wanted to. But when we're done

here, we can rush home and have sex. Ellie's at your parents' house, so–"

"No. She's not. They're at our apartment."

"What?"

"I told you they were coming to our place! Some kind of new flooring is offgassing at their house and everyone decided it would be best if they babysat here in Boston. And they're spending the night tonight."

"Oh. That changes things."

"Yes, it does."

Shannon doesn't like to have sex when she's in the same house as her parents. I don't get it.

There are these modern inventions called walls and doors. Privacy is all we need.

Proximity is Shannon's problem.

"I can't change what has already happened, Shannon." I take her hand in mine and kiss the back of it. "All I can do is rush you home. Maybe I could bang you in the back bathroom."

"*Bang* me? You call the loving conception of our second child a *bang?*"

"Yes."

She ponders for a moment, mouth twisting slightly in pensive thought, bright red lipstick glittering slightly.

Then she shrugs and says brightly, "Okay. We'll figure out the banging somehow." Those same lips that tightened a moment ago loosen with a sensual curl, her eyes meeting mine, heat rising between us in seconds.

"We absolutely will," I assure her. "Even if I end up screwing you in the back of the SUV on our way home."

Normally, that statement–in public, no less–would result in a hand swat and an admonishment from my delicious wife.

Instead, she moves closer, uses her tongue to lick a spot on my neck right under my earlobe, and whispers, "You're on."

Her hips sashay as she moves away to mingle, leaving me hard, horny, and heavily breathing through my own delighted shock. The thought of her under me in the back of the car, pulled over by the side of the road as we drive home, frenzied and desperate for each other, plays like a porn movie in my mind's eye.

"Declan?" The interruption literally shakes me, a rare startle rippling through my body.

"Yes?" I lower my voice as I turn to find Peter Mullahy before me.

"Good to see you," he says in that arch English accent he's perfected. It's close to the way the royals sound.

But not quite.

His hand stretches before me, asking for a shake. "How are you, Peter?" I ask, re-organizing my thoughts, shoving the sex images out of my head, and returning the building blocks of the CCH deal to the priority spot as I grasp his palm.

"Great. And you?" His eyes track Shannon as she walks away, making my hand tighten around his, my other arm clenching. I know that look.

He's eye-fucking my *wife*.

"Never been better."

"Excellent. I'd love to talk to you about that bid."

"Likewise."

He looks around, cunning eyes taking in the scene. Peter Mullahy is the COO of Coffee Central Holdings, a huge coffee buyer and distributor with roots going back over a hundred years. Like Anterdec, his business is a family business.

Like Anterdec, it's a Fortune 500 company.

But I'm not here representing my dad's company.

I'm representing my own.

Perfume, strong and full of a spicy floral scent I don't recognize, hits my nose before I hear Ina Mullahy's voice.

"Declan?" she asks, her hand on my shoulder as I turn.

Ina Mullahy is the heir to the CCH throne, a woman who stands at my height in heels, her regal platinum hair swept off her lightly tanned face, dark eyes penetrating.

"Ina! Nice to see you," I say with genuine affection (or something close to it). Hugs aren't required with her, and she's ten times smarter than her husband. Peter's the operations guy, out in the world shaking hands, smacking backs, and guffawing his way through deals.

"And you." She winks. "I hear we're close to making a decision on the bids. Doublann–"

"Underbid as usual and therefore will underperform," I interrupt, smiling as I speak the truth.

Knowing eyes meet mine as Peter looks behind me, bored stiff. "Money isn't everything, right?" she intones.

Ah. The biggest lie of all in a room full of people like this.

"Right," I confirm. "Long-term success rarely comes from short-term gain."

She snorts and nudges Peter. "Wish I could explain that to this big guy."

Bzzz

It's her phone. She looks down into her purse, then frowns. "Will you excuse me? We have an emergency."

"Of course," I say to empty air, Ina long gone before I finish.

A server walks by, Peter plucking a shot glass off the tray and downing what appears to be tequila in a swift move. Then he grabs another and does the same thing. A quick inventory of the man tells me he's in his cups already, quite drunk.

"Not here," he says. "How about drinks after? Or a late-night dinner? We should talk. Doublann underbid you, but we think your company is going places. You're hungrier than they are."

My gut drops. There's no true negotiation here, given how plastered he is. And no way can I go out after this affair. Heading home with Shannon is critical.

Before I can answer Peter, he gives me a boozy smile and speaks. "Great." Eyeing the bar, he moves away from me, turning back with an uncoordinated twist. "Drinks after."

Unexpectedly, Dave's at my side.

"Cyclone in Bali. It's bad. Supply chain disrupted. You need to handle this," he says to me.

"Now?" I wonder if this is why Ina departed so quickly.

"Yes." Dave nods to the right. "I've procured a small room for you. It's private. Let's go."

Bzzz

A text from Shannon. I see her across the room, the glitter of green and silver catching my eye.

Where are you? she asks. I can see her, but she can't see me.

About to deal with a problem. Cyclone in Bali, I reply.

I get a frowny face in return.

Network, I type back.

From across the room, I see her expression as she reads, her eye roll adorable, the way she licks her lips ratcheting up my need.

Soon, I add. *Soon.*

I want you desperately, she answers. *How about a quickie in the bathroom?*

My erection is ready to lead me to her like she's holding a leash. Thighs tightening, I will myself not to move, the force of my own desire so strong, I nearly sway forward.

After Bali. After Peter Mullahy, I type back as Dave gives me increasingly nonverbal cues to get out of here and into the private room for the call.

I'll take care of Mullahy. And then you'll take care of me, she responds.

Deal, I type back.

Big bangable deal.

Once I turn my attention to Bali, I spend a half hour being connected and disconnected with buyers, suppliers, and distributors half a world away. Most of the calls are about lenders and financing, so it's simple, if laborious.

Once the last fire's put out, I exit the private room, walk back into the cocktail party, and look for the smoking-hot woman in a green, glittery dress.

I spot her.

Cowering behind a guy I instantly dislike, even if I can't see his face.

There is a split second between disbelief and rage as I watch him put his hand on my wife's ass.

My.

Wife's.

Ass.

And that split second disappoints me. I should be more on the ball.

Shannon is across the room, dozens of people between us. She's off to one side of the bar, the strange man who is about to be pulverized looming over her, the guy familiar but with his head bent down, way too intimate for my tastes.

And he'd better say goodbye to that hand of his.

Because I'm about to snap it off.

As I pivot around people in the crowd, animated eyes meeting mine, lipsticked mouths opening to say hello, I change angles just enough to catch Shannon's gaze.

Panic.

Then relief at seeing me.

The guy's hand is on her hip now, touching her with unearned authority. My memory is tickled, the familiarity of the man making this even worse. That asshole thinks he has all the right in the world to give my wife a love pat.

I'll give his face a knuckle pat.

Five more steps and I'm tapping on his shoulder, using my arm to separate him from Shannon, my hand grabbing the back of his with a tight squeeze that yields bones that crunch a bit.

"I believe that ass you're groping is attached to my *wife,*" I say, voice low, blood boiling.

Damn it. It's Peter Mullahy. He's taller, thicker, and drunker than I am, but that doesn't make him the more dangerous of the two of us.

"Dec," Shannon says, the nickname telling. Breathy and a bit anxious, her voice is shorthand, going straight to my basal ganglia.

I was right.

She was upset.

"She's yours? I had no idea. You said you had a gorgeous wife, Declan, and you're right." Peter's English accent, tight and bored, greets me as I hold onto his hand, his wrist twisting against mine, trying to gain purchase. Broadening like a cobra, he swells, the half-consumed drink in his glass clearly his fifth, sixth, seventh... who knows?

His breath reeks.

"Dec, let's just go," Shannon says, pretending the guy doesn't exist. A conflict avoider, my wife doesn't appreciate the finer points of grinding a Grade-A jerk into a pulp.

"And your gorgeous wife was just telling me all the reasons why Grind It Fresh! should have our contract," he says, half his words slurred, tumbling like a mud slide off his tongue. Leering at Shannon, he tries to shake off my grip.

He fails.

"My wife is off limits." I bend his hand under, elbow twisting, ready to give him the bum's rush out of here, heedless of social niceties.

And that contract we want with CCH?

Screw it.

He recoils, face stretchy in that way only a deep drunk can manifest. "Oh, come now, I was jus' flirting." His eyes comb over Shannon as he adds in an undertone, "Besides, she's not worth fighting over. You could do better." For a nanosecond, he shoots her a condescending look.

A nanosecond is all it takes to detonate me.

"No!" Shannon gasps, lunging for my arm, her weight pulling my fist down. The unexpected maneuver makes me highly aware of the need to protect her body over the burning instinct to punch Peter in the face.

But it also gives him an opportunity, which he takes.

Knuckles have a distinct feel when they hit your jaw, more so than any other body part. On impact, the stretched skin over bone and tendon makes a scratching sound, so close to the ear, the trigeminal nerve activated as the force is absorbed by the body.

Peter comes close to executing a right hook, but it's sloppy; the impact is low, and the pain just an annoyance.

My response is not.

Street fighting wasn't part of the curriculum at Milton Academy when I went to school there, but boxing most certainly was. And while I haven't thrown a punch in years, muscle memory plus Mullahy's drunken state makes this like shooting fish in a barrel.

Rotten fish.

He's soft, the gut punch like taking aim at a thick down pillow. The guy drops, nearly falling on Shannon, but I brace myself and move to form a wall between her and the asshole. His hands clutch his bruised belly as he whines, prone on the floor.

"Like hell you're getting that contract! We're going with Doublann," he chokes out, turning red, eyes bloodshot.

I ignore him and walk away, Dave arching one eyebrow from behind a display of Alaskan crab legs. I shake my head slightly, take Shannon's arm with my non-throbbing hand, and we walk to the conference room where I just took the Bali calls.

Occupied.

"Damn," I mutter, shaking out my hand. Mutters and gasps spread through the room like a contagion as people slowly register the drama that just played out before them. Peter is standing now, glaring at hotel staff who are trying to attend to him. It's clear he's confused and angry, a bull in a china shop.

A soft bull, with no horns but plenty of tequila.

"I saw it all," Dave says under his breath, suddenly at my side. "Video will show he threw the first punch. No worries about assault charges. What the hell did he do to deserve that?"

"He put his hand on Shannon's ass."

Dave's eyes cut to her. "You okay?"

"I'm fine." Her voice is lower than I expect, more controlled and sophisticated.

I take a deep breath and look into her eyes, thinking I'll see confusion, upset, the post-crisis reaction I've observed in her over the years we've been together.

Instead, she smiles.

"Come here," I urge, leading her around the corner to a small alcove. Too many people are there, so we continue until I find a quiet spot in front of two bathrooms, both marked All Gender Restroom.

"What are you really feeling, Shannon? Because that complete and utter dick just put his hands all over you and–"

She cuts me off with a kiss.

One *hell* of a kiss.

"Dec, that was amazing," she whispers, her breath scented with the beeswax of her lipstick, the tang of white wine, the heady waft of lust. Her hands are pressed against the lapels of my jacket and her knee slides up against my thigh, roaming high, rubbing with intent.

"I... it... what?"

"You went all alpha in there."

"I'm always all alpha, Shannon."

"Not like that." Another kiss catches me off guard, but not for long. Within seconds, my hands wrap around her, fingers moving up to the nape of her neck, the kiss she initiated now mine to control. Her mouth is a playground, a gym, a training course for a competition I intend to win.

Definitively.

"You lost the contract," she gasps as my hand slides up her leg, under her skirt, finding her without panties.

"I like this," I reply, my finger moving in just the right place, making her moan against my ear as I back her against the wall.

"We can't!" she murmurs. "Not here."

She's morally right.

But technically wrong.

I sure as hell *can*.

5

Declan

INSTEAD OF HAVING A QUICKIE IN THE HALLWAY, I grab the handle to one of the bathrooms and pull her in, clicking the lock with a Shannon-scented hand.

"We can, in here," I say as I begin stripping off my jacket, the need to be inside her so strong, I can't control it. Her eyes, her face, the flush of her skin as she breathes heavily, chest rising and falling with that plunging neckline, the green and silver turning her into a moveable feast–I have to feel her warmth.

Have to touch her *power*.

She reaches for my belt, unloops it, unzips my pants, and in a second, she lifts her leg, pressing one shoe against the tiled wall, her hand guiding me inside her. The citrus and spice of her perfume blends with the taste of her, our mouths hungry and hard, every sense co-mingling until she's moaning against my mouth, her fingers digging into my hips, begging for more.

I pound into her, the thrusts designed to make me stop thinking, to crush her into the wall as she whispers obscene, filthy words in my ear. The rough and ready way my wife is treating my body is as much a thrill as the actual sex.

And then I come.

It's fast, the burst exploding through me, the rush like no other. I keep going, her body tight, her heel scraping the back of my knee as she tenses and throws her head back against the wall. Bending down, I scoop one breast out of the top of her dress and kiss her nipple, sucking and biting until she clenches around me and–oh.

Oh.

So deep, I can't believe there's more, I push into her as she makes a soundless noise, the way she pulls inward its own separate, arousing plane of existence. Caught up in herself completely as my body is immersed in hers, she's here but gone, sent to an emotion and a visceral feeling I can't experience with her.

But I can make her feel it.

Me.

Only *me*.

One bite, a snap that I know will drive pleasure through her as much as it ripples pain, is all it takes for her to nearly sing as I slowly, achingly slowly, thrust into her one last time. Her body shudders with a delicious joy that makes her skin smell like ecstasy.

And then she slumps against me, laughing.

"I guess," she says between breaths, panting, "we made it within that ovulation window after all."

Her words wash over me, and I make a sound that I hope is close enough to a laugh. I can't form verbal strings quite yet, so profound was the transformation from two to one. Shannon doesn't do this kind of public sex.

But obviously that's not true any longer.

An embarrassed laugh titters out of my wife, shaking me into language again.

"Hey," I say, touching her chin with my fingers. Her eyes don't want to meet mine, full of a sudden modesty. Unleashed and unmoored, she unveils new parts of herself to me.

All those layers of beauty make spending forever together so exciting.

"Shannon," I say, her eyes lifting up to meet mine.

"Mmm?"

"That was amazing. More, please."

Alarm flashes in her eyes. "Now?"

"No. But... later."

"I won't be ovulating later."

"I don't care."

Her arms wrap around me, cheek resting on my shoulder as I shift my hips and slide out, her leg dropping.

"Dec?"

"Yes?"

"I love you."

"I know."

"And that guy? Peter?"

My shoulders broaden, my anger a reminder of my sore knuckles, which I hold up to view.

"Yeah?"

"He's the guy who decides on who wins the contract, yes?"

"Yes."

"I'm–"

Before the words are out of her mouth, I kiss her. "No," I whisper fiercely. "You don't get to say you're sorry. You did nothing wrong. He's one-hundred percent responsible for his transgression."

For the next minute, we clean ourselves up in silence. Shannon sneaks little glances at me, an impish, pleased look about her. I straighten my pants, close up shop, wash my hands, and align my tie.

"Ready?" we ask each other in unison.

And then we go back to the gathering, pretending we didn't just screw each other's brains out in a single-stall bathroom at a charity fundraiser.

Immediately, we're joined by Dave, who taps on his phone without looking up. I swear he mutters something about conception attempt number one, but that can't be right.

"Damage control in place," Dave informs me in *sotto voce*. "But watch out at two o'clock."

I glance in that direction and see Peter Mullahy approaching, a hangdog look on his red face. "Look, let's keep this under wraps. Here's the cover story," he says, not making eye contact, words still slurred. "We were joking around. Wrestling. It got out of hand and–"

"Get the hell away from me." I cut him off, moving my body between him and Shannon.

"You get the deal," he says in a dark, low voice. "Keep this quiet and you get the deal."

"Absolutely not," I snap.

Shannon's hand goes to my elbow, her touch firm. With a single glance, she tells me she's got this.

"We'll take the job, but our bid has now increased ten percent," she says coolly, staring him down.

I'm impressed. Even *I* didn't think of that.

He stares at her. "You can't do that!"

"She most certainly can," says Ina, who has appeared, joined our little group, and instantly assessed the situation. She looks at Shannon and says, "I apologize on behalf of my husband."

"Ina," he says in a hybrid of condescension and pleading, "you can't let them blackmail me into a more expensive contract just because a little roughhousing got out of hand!"

Dave holds up his phone. We all turn. He hits Play.

It shows security footage of the moments just before I found Shannon being harassed by Peter.

The hand on her ass is clear.

"Where did you get that? It's doctored! It's–"

Ina cuts Peter off and, bypassing me, turns to Shannon. "I won't automatically agree to the ten percent increase, but I would like to take you out to lunch to discuss terms for possibly working together." She cuts Peter a scathing look. "My husband will *not* be managing this project."

"Ina," Peter says in a low growl. "You can't–"

"As the majority shareholder in the corporation, I just *did*, Peter." Grabbing his arm, she yanks him, his loose muscles making him stumble. "Call me, Shannon. Declan's assistant has my number." She gives Dave a nod. "And an impressive set of tech skills. Interested in working for CCH?"

"No," Dave replies, eyelid twitching. I know what that means.

I nearly groan. Great. Another raise for Dave.

A philosophical smile backed by steel is the last we see from Ina before she turns away, frog-marching Peter toward the elevators, the tongue lashing evident.

"Whew!" Shannon says, shoulders dropping, hip leaning against the wall. "That was intense."

My wife has never been hotter. Ever. Not once. Watching her negotiate like that has me hard again.

Dave looks at his phone. "Gotta go." He disappears.

Good man.

"That was *amazing*," I correct her, coming in for a kiss. "How did you know to do that?"

"I learned from the best." She pats my cheek.

"Shannon, let's go home."

"Home? Now? I thought–"

I push the elevator button and give her a long, wet, slow kiss. "Home. Let's go home."

6

Declan

15 DAYS LATER

SHANNON PADS OUT OF THE BATHROOM HOLDING A pregnancy test, face twisted with disappointment.

"Negative," she declares, unnecessarily, as she shakes her head. It's the same kind of test she took this morning. We know she didn't conceive, so why can't she let it go and move on?

Actually, I know why. We've been married for five years. The question is rhetorical.

The disappointment isn't.

Ellie's finally gone to bed, the stubborn new tooth that's prying its way through her gums the bane of our existence these days. It's dark outside, the moon low in the sky and covered by clouds. The night feels different than normal, Shannon's wistful gaze at the pregnancy test making it harder to breathe for some reason. A snowflake catches my eye, then another, the reminder that Christmas is just two weeks away making me cringe.

Because the holiday two years ago wasn't exactly calm. I look at Shannon's cat, Chuckles, who gives me a flat look back that says, *That's right, buddy. I set the Christmas tree on fire two years ago. I gave you a year's reprieve. Piss me off enough, and I'll do it again.*

Then he walks out of the room, butthole on full display.

"It's our first try," I remind Shannon, looking away from the cat. I pat the cold side of the bed next to me. "We'll just have to keep trying."

"Quit grinning when you say that."

"Am I grinning? I had no idea."

"I thought you hated failure."

"Who said I failed?"

"We're not pregnant. That means we failed."

"If getting pregnant on the first try is the goal, then yes, we failed. If spending month after month paying delicious attention to your beautiful body as we try to make another amazing baby is the goal, then I'm wildly succeeding."

Before she can say another word, I lunge, pulling her to the bed by her waist. Her squeals of protest dissolve into moans as I kiss her, and the White Plastic Stick of Judgment drops to the ground, where it belongs. We both want our kids to be close enough in age to be playmates, but Shannon's definitely more concerned about conceiving quickly.

A role reversal, for sure. Normally, I'm the driven one, anxious to close the deal, eager for success.

But I also know what pregnancy does to my wife, and if there's a way to enjoy her in these intimate moments with a little more frequency before doubling our child capacity, I'll take it.

Bzzz

We both groan.

"Mine," she says, rolling onto her tummy and reaching over me to grab her phone. She squints at the screen.

"It's Dad. He says he'll be here at 5 a.m. tomorrow to pick you up, with Andrew, then you'll head up to Maine with the troop."

I groan. "I can't believe they roped me into this." My father-in-law asked me to come along as a chaperone for a Boy Scouts trip to Maine with our nephews Tyler and Jeffrey, to collect holiday wreaths for the annual troop sale. Apparently, the troop ran out and there's so much demand, they need to make the extra run to restock and earn more money for a big scouting trip in the future.

"*I* can't believe you said yes!"

"Your dad asked us. And you told me a while ago that you wanted me to spend more time with him." I don't mention the added incentive of possible blueberry beer. I'm guessing Jason wants more adults to attend so he can swing by his favorite brewery, grab ten cases at a discount, and bring them home.

"True. I'm just surprised you agreed."

"First of all, I like your dad."

A gimlet eye I deserve shoots my way.

"Okay. Fine. Andrew said yes. I had to. Can't have him holding this over me. I have no idea why he agreed to go."

Shannon snorts. "I know why. Amanda told me. He wants to test out being a father."

"He *is* a father! They have twins!" I think for a few seconds. "Huh. There's your answer."

"What?"

"He has two babies at home. This will be a *vacation* for him."

"Andrew doesn't need to come up with excuses to get away from Amanda and the boys."

"No, but this is a really good one. Helping your dad, who she adores, and going away on a Boy Scout trip? It'll trigger her imagination to think into the future about a time when their babies are little boys. Andrew gets *major* brownie points for this."

I can't admit I'm impressed, but my little brother has mad skills.

"Boy Scout points. You're the one who will earn Brownie points."

"What do you mean?"

"When Ellie's old enough, she'll join Brownie scouts."

"Brownie what?"

"You know. *Brownies*. That's what they call little girls before they become Girl Scouts. Like Cub Scouts become Boy Scouts."

"I didn't know that."

"Do you live under a rock?"

"I get the feeling if this conversation goes on much longer, I will be."

Bzzz

"My turn," I mutter as I feel for my phone, groping blindly behind me until I knock it off the table. Shannon giggles and I twist, then slide half off the bed, a smack on my bare ass well deserved.

The glowing screen simply says, *See you at five a.m. Wear long johns.*

"Long johns? Who says 'long johns' anymore?"

"My dad."

"Was his language frozen in 1962?"

"Do you have the silk long johns Mom got you for Christmas a few years ago?"

"Somewhere, sure. I wear them when we ski."

"When was the last time we skied?" Tilting her head, she looks up at me, eyes questioning.

"When we went to..." My mind goes blank. When did we last ski?

"Ever since we had Ellie, we've stopped doing so many things," Shannon says with a funny look on her face.

"We've added plenty of others," I point out. "Like bathtimes, hair-combing wrestling matches, and my personal favorite: Five thousand renditions of *Itsy Bitsy Spider*."

"That's *so* not the same as a four-day weekend in Aspen." Her gaze cuts to the pregnancy test, brow dropping.

"We should go away. Just the two of us." Stroking her arm, I let her mood sink in, changing my words on the fly as I realize what's going on. "You're worried that adding a baby will take even more time away from the fun stuff we used to do."

"It's not about the fun stuff. It's about having less time with you."

"Me? Since when did I become important?" I joke, but the humor doesn't work on her.

"That's just it, Dec." Shining eyes meet mine. Damn. "I don't make you important. We don't ski anymore. We hardly ever go to plays or concerts together. Even charity events are hit-or-miss now that we have Ellie. All we do is work and raise her."

"And that's not enough for you."

"It's more than enough! That's the problem."

"Too much scope? We can solve that. Rely on nannies more. Take some things off your plate at work." Pulling her in, we snuggle, my nose burying in her hair. A faint whiff of herbs and vanilla, of Shannon's natural skin, fills my senses.

"It feels so big, I can't break it down like that."

"What do you mean? Any problem can be broken down and solved step by step."

"Are you sure?"

"Yes."

"What makes you so sure?"

"I just am."

A long, amused sigh comes out of her, the hot breath tickling my bare chest. "That's part of what I admire about you, Declan. That certainty."

"I believe you called it stubbornness the other night, when I refused to go thrift shopping with your mom for that stupid Yankee Swap tradition."

"That *was* stubbornness! And it's different."

"How is it different?"

"Because there's a huge difference between self-assurance and being intractable."

"That's true."

"So you *will* go thrift shopping with Mom?"

"No."

"Dec," she groans.

"Admire my certainty, Shannon," I whisper as my hand moves between her legs, finding the soft, sweet curves that I am absolutely certain are perfection itself.

Her hand finds me hard. "This is definitely hard headed." Her palm rides up to the tip. I inhale sharply, her scent piercing my awareness, the need to kiss her too great to ignore.

Her mouth finds mine, both of us seeking the same as we become a tumble of sheets, discarded pajamas, and sensual intentions. Between my wife's legs, I find a place of excitement, of passion, of comfort, of–

"MAMAMAMAMAMAMAMAMA!" Ellie screams through the intercom, making Shannon sit up fast in surprise, her forehead connecting with my chin. I bite down hard, trapping my lip between my teeth.

"Muvafuffer," I lisp, the copper-sweet taste of my own blood adding injury to insult. Touching the wound doesn't make it any better as Shannon wiggles out from under me, face flushed, mouth in an uninjured pout.

"And we want *more*?" she mutters as she stands, pawing through the twisted sheets to find her nightgown, which she yanks on.

Within seconds, she looks like an octopus caught in a net.

"What the...?" The hem around her neck, she grits her teeth and mutters a curse. In her haste, she's put her head through the wrong opening. Normally, I'd laugh, but my lip is swelling rapidly. Between this and the fading bruise from Peter Mullahy's badly-aimed punch two weeks ago, I'm starting to look like I got rolled in an alley.

All the blood that was just in my cock seems to be migrating north, the throb below the waist turning into the throb I hate to taste.

"I want UP! I want UP!"

As Shannon wrestles with her nightgown like she's pinning an alligator, I lick my wound, literally, and go to find Ellie in her room. Her eyes glisten in the nightlight's glow, arms reaching for me to lift her out of her crib.

She immediately curls her head under my collarbone, closes her eyes, and sniffs rhythmically.

Unlike my wife, I actually agree with the night nurse we used on and off (more off than I'd have liked) for Ellie's first year, and I don't bring our toddler into the bed on nights like this. The night nurse recommended putting a chaise longue in her bedroom as a reading nook/temporary sleeping surface for the parent who soothes, and I go to it, stretching out for the few minutes it'll take until Ellie sleeps soundly enough to transfer back to her crib.

"*Shhh,*" I whisper as she whimpers, dark, silky curls brushing against my slightly swollen lip. She smells like baby soap and innocent youth.

For the next few minutes, I take deep, slow breaths, knowing I can influence her with my calmness, lull her into a sleep trance, and get back to my wife as fast as possible. These precious minutes of the night tick by fast, and I have a 4 a.m. wake-up time.

My wife's back in our bed, curled up and waiting for me.

Taming a toddler's sleep patterns is easy.

So easy.

So... eeee...

Zzzz

❧

"DEC? DEC? DAD'S DOWNSTAIRS."

"Huh?" I jolt, weight slipping off me, Shannon grabbing a sound-asleep Ellie before my reflexes can snap to it.

"You fell asleep with her on the chaise," she explains in a whisper, thrusting something silky onto my bare chest. "Dad's downstairs with Andrew and the scouts."

"The who?"

"The scouts? Remember? Five a.m.?"

"It's five already?"

"*Shhhh.*" As Shannon gently peels Ellie out of my arms, the silky thing falls limply to the floor.

Long johns.

Watching my wife bend over Ellie's crib helps wake up part of me. Her fine ass shows off curves that my admiring eyes transmit to other parts of me, parts that want to do more than admire.

Instead, I reach down for the long johns and shove my feet in.

Three minutes later, I'm in full winter gear, Shannon's hastily made thermos of coffee a welcome addition to my rushed exit.

"Love you," she whispers as I get a kiss on the cheek. "Have fun."

All I can do is grab her ass, grunt, and leave.

The white van is a huge fourteen-seater with a big cargo section in the back. It idles in front of our building while the doorman, Barry, chats amiably with my father-in-law. I head to the passenger's seat with a yawn, only to find a very familiar face occupying my space.

My little brother.

Tap tap tap

"Move it," I order, giving him a thumb gesture.

He snorts and thumbs me toward the back.

My thumb turns into a different finger I point at him.

Too tired to argue, I grab the handle for the back and open it to find four kids, ranging in age from about ten to teenager, all bent over electronic devices of some kind.

They all look up in unison.

"Declan!" Jeffrey calls out. "I told you guys! Two billionaires in one van!"

"That's *one* billionaire," Andrew corrects him. "Your uncle doesn't have a net worth of a billion."

Jason turns up the radio, Boston's "More Than a Feeling" blasting through the speakers as he pulls away from my building and heads toward the entrance to I-93 North.

"You don't?"

Jeffrey's shouted question cuts through my gut like a knife. Investing an enormous chunk of my net worth into Grind It Fresh! Means that technically, I've lost billionaire status. Leveraged comfortably, I'm poised to exceed my father's financial accomplishments.

But not quite yet.

"Neither does he," I point out. Andrew resigned from his CEO position at Anterdec last May. Dad hasn't spoken to him since.

I have to admit I'm envious.

"I absolutely do," Andrew argues. "I'm vested enough and I have plenty. Being CEO all these years paid off."

"'All these years'? You were CEO for five years! That's it."

"That was enough." Smug eyes meet mine.

"I can't believe you two are fighting about this," Jason cuts in, thumbing toward the back of the van. "Fine role models you are. I asked you to be chaperones with me to meet Scouting regulations and to expose the scouts to business-savvy adults."

"Is that why you invited us? To be role models?" Andrew asks. Jeffrey snorts with a tone that reminds me he is, without question, firmly a teenager, even if he's only thirteen.

I expect Jason to reply in the affirmative, but instead, he gives me a shifty-eyed response reminiscent of his wife.

Which sets the hair on the back of my neck at attention.

"Jason," I ask sharply as he notches up the volume on the radio again, "why *did* you invite us?" I'm starting to suspect no blueberry beer is forthcoming.

He cups his hand over his ear and shrugs as if to say, *Oh, well. Can't hear you. Conversation over.*

I kill the radio.

"Why did you invite us?" I repeat.

He clears his throat and says, "To chaperone. To help."

"You couldn't get any other parents to come along?"

His pause reminds me what a terrible liar the man is. Now I understand why he's never made it in the corporate world.

"I–I thought you and Andrew were a better fit."

My brother's eyes catch mine.

We lean closer to Jason.

"What exactly does that mean?" Andrew asks.

"Oh, you know. You have little kids. You need a break from the craziness at home. Isn't it nice not to have your eardrums shredded by crying?" he asks affably. Is that a thin sheen of sweat forming along his receding hairline?

"Jason." I use a tone designed to make the sweat increase.

It works.

Remind me never to ask this guy to lie for me. Or negotiate a hostage situation.

Or even haggle at a lemonade stand.

"You two need a glimpse into the future," he says as we reach the New Hampshire state line, the GPS announcing our crossing of the border in a flat female voice.

Fart noises begin from the back row.

"Or the past," Andrew says with a grin. "This does remind me of the bus to swim meets when we were at Milton."

"And soccer," I admit as I overhear conversation about Cardi B's boobs. Jason told me there are strict rules about Scouting trips.

No phones or electronics – the kids are on them.

No discussions about sex – but I hear them whispering about Cardi B.

Two or more adults chaperoning, and never alone with a single scout.

So far, we're one for three.

"See?" Jason whooshes with relief. "That's what I mean. Getting you two around kids and getting used to this way of spending time."

"Time?" Andrew and I ask in unison.

"Sure. Time. You guys have a different perception of how to spend time."

"We do?"

"Isn't it obvious?"

"If it were, we'd understand what you're talking about."

"For you, time is money."

Andrew and I frown at the same time, eyes roving left and right, processing Jason's words.

I tilt my head and give my brother a look that says, *Do you know what he's talking about?*

I'm answered with a shrug.

"Time *is* money," I finally venture, as if Jason has just declared the Earth is flat.

"See? That's what I mean. Your dad taught you that."

"What does our father have to do with this?"

"Did James ever take you on a Boy Scout trip like this?"

Booming laughter from me and my brother fills the van, mingling with the fart noises in the back to create a new kind of soundtrack.

A self-satisfied grin covers Jason's face. It's a look I've never seen on him before.

"See? He didn't."

"His limo driver brought him to the finals if our teams made it," I point out. "But only for the finals."

"He was at my swim meets," Andrew counters.

"All of them? Or just the finals?"

"Fair enough."

"Did he ever just... spend time with you? Hang out?"

We shake our heads.

"He taught you that time had to have a purpose, and the purpose was money."

"Or achievement," Andrew adds, as if the variety matters.

We nod soberly. My brother, my father-in-law, and I are caught up in this impromptu therapy session with a backdrop of juicy shart sounds.

The kids in the back have upped the ante.

And suddenly, they're chanting the famous "Diarrhea" song from summer camps everywhere. "*When you're sliding into third, and you feel a juicy turd–*"

"SCOUTS!" Jason shouts to the back.

They halt, hushed giggles replacing the line about turds. It reminds me of the Turdmobile, and I take out my phone and text Dave:

If we donate the Turdmobile to a charity, is there any way to get good PR without being humiliated?

His one-word response does not surprise me:

No.

I tuck the phone back into my pocket as Jordan takes their earbuds out and calmly, almost primly, says, "For the record, Mr. Jacoby, I wasn't singing."

"Thank you, Jordan."

"I have IBS and find that song to be offensive. It's making fun of differently abled, digestively challenged Americans."

The van goes quiet.

"Digestively challenged?" Andrew mouths to me.

Two resonant fart sounds punctuate the air, faces covered with ski caps or buried in phones.

Jason turns up the volume again. Any louder and the radio will vibrate us a foot off the asphalt.

The Piscataqua River Bridge is a mighty arch that carries us over the water as we leave the corner of New Hampshire we crossed through on I-95.

"Which way do you want us to piss?" Steegan shouts.

"PISCATA-WAY!" Jeffrey calls back, the two a pile of giggles as Jason gives them a glare in the rearview mirror.

Tyler starts repeating, "Piss cat! Piss cat!"

"Guys," Jason says in a warning tone, shutting them down to giggles.

And soon the GPS is telling us we're in Maine.

The female voice is mighty bored by it, too.

"Nice deflection, and the Scouts' digestive jokes helped," Andrew says to Jason as he opens a thermos of coffee and takes a huge gulp. "But why are we really here?"

Instead of the shifty eyes, Jason's lower lids squint up slowly, like Clint Eastwood in an old western. "Why do you think there's some reason other than chaperoning?"

"Cut the crap, Jason. I don't like being manipulated. You're reminding me of Dad now," Andrew says in a firm voice.

"Me? Like James? You've got to be kidding me."

"Something about this stinks."

Pffft pffft comes the soundtrack to Andrew's overheard comment.

I turn around to find Tyler with his palms pressed to his face, wrists in the center of his lips and fingers wrapped around his jaw, blowing air to make fart sounds.

Jeffrey's tutoring is paying off.

"YES!" he shouts to Tyler, offering a high five as Tyler nervously completes the ritual. He's obviously unsure whether to be pleased with himself or not, but he'll take the positive attention from his brother anyhow.

Given that Jason is still avoiding our question, Andrew tries a different tack.

"This entire trip has me confused. Why not just pay someone to deliver the wreaths?" he asks, the question a poke.

One that I recognize as a negotiation tactic, but Jason takes at face value.

"We're teaching the boys the value of hard work."

"You're teaching them to waste their time."

"Excuse me?"

"This." Andrew waves his hand. "This is teaching them to be *workers*, not entrepreneurs."

He reminds me of Dad, down to the wrist pop.

Jason arches a disapproving eyebrow, a sternness coming over him that I don't normally see. "They're buying wholesale, and we're selling at retail. They'll see the profit. Every step of the way, the kids are learning how to make money for the troop to fund activities. This is our second trip for supplies. We sold out because the kids hustled."

Andrew's mouth tightens before he asks, "What are they selling other than wreaths?"

"That's it. Just wreaths."

"No Christmas trees?" Andrew is skeptical. At the words *Christmas trees,* though, Jason turns a funny shade of red, breaking eye contact.

Hmmm.

"A different troop in the area has the tree booth." Now Jason's stare is flat and even. It's clear Andrew expects him to back down, but my father-in-law isn't the type. He's no alpha, but Jason Jacoby can hold his own when a principle is at stake.

He might not be able to lie worth a damn, but he can maintain integrity like no one else.

"What about high-profit items, like refreshments? Or buying cheap holiday ornaments from China and selling them at the wreath stand?" Andrew's tone is flat, like he's reciting the obvious.

"That's not how this works."

"Why not?"

"It's not how we've done it all these years."

"Then shake it up! Teach them how true capitalism works."

Jason's beginning to look like he *really* regrets inviting Andrew.

Which is Andrew's point. Create chaos inside the guy, then go in for the kill.

"They're kids, Andrew. Running a wreath stand in a bank parking lot on the weekends. We're not beholden to shareholders who expect quarterly growth. This isn't Anterdec."

"The founder of the next Anterdec could be a Boy Scout, Jason. How do you expect the next generation to understand how to grow a business and maximize profits if you don't teach them the basic principles?"

"Most of these kids can't remember to zip their flies after going to the bathroom. You expect them to run a profit and loss sheet with an eye on a higher asymptotic growth curve?" Jason says in a low, amused voice.

Jason's dismissal of Andrew's passion hits a nerve.

"Grandpa?" Jeffrey pipes up from the middle row. Jason's eyes cut to the rearview mirror, looking grateful for the interruption.

"Yeah?"

"Andrew's got a point. Selling popcorn and wreaths every year isn't earning us a lot of money. What if we add something else? Something that'll get us more customers?"

"We have plenty of customers," Jason replies patiently. "We always sell out of the wreaths and here we are, getting a whole extra van of them."

"How many days do you have the lot?" Andrew asks, twisting in his seat to ask Jeffrey.

"Four more."

"Which means you could easily sell even more, and make more money."

"Actually," Jeffrey says, pulling out his smartphone, "if we sold something more than wreaths, and sold everything across all four days, we'd exceed past profit records. Hey, Steegan–what else could we sell?"

Steegan looks up from his phone and shrugs. "I don't know. Candy?"

"We can't sell candy," Jason explains. "Other troops sell candy, and there's a candy store three blocks away. We have agreements with local businesses, and–"

"What about coffee?" Jordan asks, giving Andrew an eager look. "Most of our customers are moms in minivans and old people. They love coffee."

"My mom loves coffee," Steegan says in a bored voice. "Dad says she needs to have an affair with someone who works at Starbucks so she can get it at a discount."

The word Starbucks makes Andrew smirk at me. I loathe that word.

I reach into my wallet and pull out a card. "Here. Give this to your mom. It'll give her a discount on much better coffee than that toilet water masquerading as coffee."

Steegan gives me major side eye. "I'm not collecting phone numbers for my mom to have an affair."

"EWWWWW!" Jeffrey squeals, hitting three different octaves. "He's not trying to bang your mom! Uncle Declan would never do that."

Andrew is now folded over in half, shaking silently, shoulders bouncing up and down.

"BOYS!" Jason bellows.

Jordan clears their throat.

"Uh, and–Jordan."

Primly, the kid looks at him and says, "You can use the plural noun 'scouts' to refer to us as a group, Mr. Jacoby." They look at Jeffrey and whisper, "I think your grandpa is upset you're talking about banging. The grown-ups like to think we don't know anything about sex."

"Grown-ups?" Andrew nudges me. "*We're* the grown-ups now?"

"You're finally figuring that out?"

"BANG! Uncle Declan's banging!" Tyler shouts. "Bang bang bang!"

"How long's the drive?" I ask Jason, who points to the GPS.

One hour, four minutes.

"BANG YOUR MOM!" Tyler calls out. "BANG YOUR MOM!"

"Tyler," Jeffrey says gently. "You're repeating."

Tyler goes silent.

Jason's mouth moves from grim determination to tender recognition.

"I'd like silence in here, everyone. No sex talk, no screaming. Just... a few moments to do those meditative breathing exercises we learned about from that yoga class we took last year at one of our meetings."

The silence continues. I'm surprised, and I see why Jason is pleased. Tyler is eleven and has a neurological language disorder, along with auditory processing issues. In modern terms, he has special needs that don't fit easily into any one box. Jason volunteered to be Boy Scout leader in part because he wanted to have an informed adult supervising Tyler's journey through scouting.

And being able to cut through Tyler's repetitive speech with a gentle comment that makes Tyler more aware–and that he's able to stop–is huge progress.

Steegan's brow is down, eyes blinking rapidly. He looks up, clears his throat, and asks, "Mr. Jacoby?"

"Yes?"

"What does bang your mom mean? Is it like banging a drum? Because that would mean hitting her, and I don't think anyone should hit a mom."

"No one bangs a mom," Tyler says, unexpectedly somber. "That would hurt! That would be bad."

The van goes silent again, Jeffrey and Jordan looking toward Jason, Jeffrey's impish smile making me feel very young again.

As the seconds tick on, Jason opens his mouth, shuts it, opens it again, presses the accelerator until the van hits 73 miles per hour, and closes his mouth again with a long sigh.

"Steegan?" he finally asks.

"Yes?"

"Make you a deal. Declan has a bag of chocolates under his seat." He gestures for me to find it. I do, pulling out a small reusable shopping bag from a regional grocery store chain. "Let's have our first round of treats."

"Okay. But what does bang your mom really mean?"

Jeffrey leans over and whispers the thirteen-year-old boy version of an answer to that question.

Steegan's eyes get huge.

Then he looks away and mutters, "Bang means screw? Why didn't you just say so?"

"I didn't say screw!" Jeffrey protests. "I said fu–"

"SCOUTS!" Jason, Andrew, and I shout in unison.

Jason blasts the AC/DC song that serendipitously comes on the radio just then, flurries picking up speed as the van does, too.

I really am one of the grown-ups.

Even if it doesn't feel like it.

By the time the AC/DC song ends, the troop members have gone back to fart noises and arguments about Roblox and Fortnite, which leads Andrew to ask:

"Are those blockchain currencies?"

"They're video games," I say loudly, expecting laughter from the scouts.

Instead, Jeffrey leans in and says to Andrew, "No, but I wanted to ask you about crypto-currency. Ever heard of Russian doubloons?"

"No." Andrew frowns. "Should I?"

"Yes!" Jeffrey stretches his jaw forward in an expression of disbelief, eyes bugged out. "Billionaires could become trillionaires if they invest in them."

"That so?"

"That so?" Jeffrey mimics, making Andrew's jaw clench. "I'm giving you a hot tip."

"You're eleven, right?"

"Thirteen."

"Whatever. I don't take my investment advice from seventh graders."

"Maybe you should, Boomer."

Jason bursts out laughing.

"Your grandfather is a Boomer, kid. I'm a Millennial," Andrew scoffs. "You're not even a Zoomer. What're you? Other than a zygote."

"I'm a kid who knows a lot about 4chan and how to use TikTok as a viral weapon."

Andrew picks up his phone and starts texting. "Fine. I'll ask my investment team what they think. Can't hurt to pick up a few shares of this Russian doubloon thing. How much are they?"

"Eleven cents each."

"*Pffft*. I'll buy a hundred thousand."

The gleam in Jeffrey's eye turns me suspicious.

"How many shares do *you* own?" I ask him.

"A thousand."

"That's a $110 investment." I nudge my brother. "You can buy a few million."

Jeffrey looks like he's salivating.

"How did you come across that kind of money?" I ask Jeffrey. $110 is a cheap haircut for Andrew and me, but for Jeffrey, it's an enormous sum.

"I earned it mowing lawns and cleaning Grandpa's man cave."

I cut to my father-in-law. "Not the Coffee Can of Doom?"

Jeffrey begins to gag.

"Why can't you just pee on a bush like the rest of us?" I challenge Jason, who shakes his head.

"I don't use it for that!"

"Pee on a bush!" Tyler says before Jeffrey calmly sets his hand on his shoulder, stopping the kid from repeating himself. Tyler frowns, eyebrows turning down, before he looks at me and asks, "Why not pee on a flower?"

Jason cranks the music up, but it doesn't deter Jeffrey, who pokes Andrew's elbow and asks, "What's your threshold for investment? What kind of ROI do you want to see before you take a chance?"

Great. I'm the guy being asked about peeing on flowers, while my brother's being pumped for financial advice from a kid who still wears braces.

"You're the real billionaire, right?" Jordan asks, plucking one earbud out, eyes on Andrew.

"Hey!" I snap.

Jordan's eyebrow judges me. "Can't escape reality, sir. Numbers don't lie."

The *sir* is icing on the ego-pop cake.

"Jordan's right, *sir*," Andrew says to me, clearly enjoying this. "And yes, I'm the real billionaire in this van. What do you want to know?"

"How does your conscience let you sleep at night when there are so many homeless and poor people in the world who don't even have food or a safe place to sleep, while you have so much?"

Andrew just blinks.

I motion toward him with the hands of a game show assistant. "Go ahead, everyone. Ask the billionaire anything."

"Shut up," he mutters under his breath to me. He turns to Jordan with a charming smile that works on women, but I don't think a woke nonbinary teenager is going to be snowed.

"Guys–er, scouts–be kind and respectful to Mr. McCormick. His company has donated millions of dollars to important causes," Jason says in a voice that makes it clear we're all walking some careful lines here.

"Like climate change?" Jordan perks up.

"Sure," Andrew says, nodding slowly. I know damn well he has no idea which causes Anterdec donates to. His executive assistant, Gina, does.

Andrew just shows up at the charity events for photos and networking.

Then again, I can't cast stones from my glass house.

I was the same way until I bought my own company.

"Like what?" Steegan presses.

"Like what... what?"

"Like what causes?"

"Oh, you know..."

"No. We don't. That's why we're asking. You know, you Boomers ruined the Earth for our generation. And billionaires like you are making it even worse. You owe us, Mr. McCormick," Jordan says solemnly.

"First of all, Boomers are people born between 1946 and 1965. I'm not *that* old."

"You look like you could have been born in 1965," Steegan adds helpfully, studying my brother.

"That would make me fifty-five! I'm not ancient."

"HEY!" Jason bellows.

"The only Boomer in this van is Mr. Jacoby," I start to explain.

"He's a good Boomer," Jordan says with obvious affection for their scout leader. "Not like the rest of you."

"We're not Boomers!" Why Andrew has picked this battle to fight is beyond me.

"Fine. Whatever. You're not Boomers." Jordan's not convinced. "But you are rich. And you hoard your money and make it harder for the rest of the people to live good lives."

"Who taught you this–?" Andrew demands. He cuts himself off before saying the word crap.

Or worse.

"Everyone! My parents, my minister, my teachers. We're learning about political economy and the history of taxation in my geography and American government classes."

"Then you're also learning about capitalism," Andrew says smoothly.

"Yes. And people like you exploit the working classes to extract value and hoard it."

A lightbulb goes off in Andrew's head. "You just read the *Communist Manifesto*, didn't you?"

Jordan nods.

"Careful," Jason warns, drawing the word out. I'm not sure if it's aimed at Andrew or Jordan.

Or both.

"Heya! We're five minutes away! And look at the snow," Jason says loudly.

The guy is a master at deflection, the kids soon pressing their noses against the windows, eagerly watching the flakes fly, visions of Santa – who looks a little like Karl Marx – dancing in their heads.

Jason still hasn't answered our question about why he picked me and Andrew for this trip.

As Jason exits the highway, I'm surprised a Christmas tree and wreath farm is so close, but five minutes turns out to be optimistic. Fifteen minutes of back-country roads later, we turn onto a white-dusted dirt road that makes the van rock back and forth as we hit rut after rut.

The kids make a game of it, exaggerating the jostling, slamming their bodies into each other, until Tyler starts screaming, "You will NOT! You will NOT!"

But they ignore him.

Jason pulls the van up to an enormous barn with smoke floating out of a chimney pipe on the right wall, the wooden structure leaning slightly away from the smoke as if trying to escape it. Like so many farms in Maine, this barn has seen better days, but it's clearly still functional. Row after row of fat Balsam firs line up neatly as far as the eye can see, all of them wearing caps of snow on the peaks.

As Jason puts the van in park and kills the engine, there's a scuffle of kids pulling on hats and gloves. Andrew chugs his coffee, while Jason cranes to look around.

"Scouts!" he calls out. "Remember, we'll need lots of room in the back. On the way home, you can't spread out in the last rows. We'll have boxes of wreaths in there."

I point to a bag filled with twine. "Why not tie everything to the roof? There's a rack."

Jason's eyes gleam. "I have other plans for the roof." Rubbing his palms together, he looks like an over-the-top villain in a cartoon.

"Huh?"

"I'll show you."

Hmm. We're about to find out why Andrew and I are really here, aren't we?

Finally.

"Jason!" a man in an actual raccoon-fur hat ambles over, long and lean with an old Yankee look, but he can't be more than my age. He has sharp blue eyes and overgrown blonde hair that curls around his ears under his thick wool cap. His teeth are crooked when he smiles, and the death grip he has on Jason's hand, other hand on his shoulder, tells me they're longtime friends. "Been a long time! Bring the whole troop?"

"Not this time. There's an indoor soccer tournament this weekend, so half of them couldn't come."

The guy eyes me up and down, face closing off the way northern New Englanders often do when confronted with a stranger. "Heya. I'm Perlman." His offered hand is like shaking a steel cable.

"Hi, Perlman. I'm Declan." His eyes cut to Andrew, who goes through the same handshake.

"Declan?" Those blue eyes cut to me. "You the billionaire who got lucky enough to snag Shannon?"

Wasn't expecting *that*.

"You know my wife?"

Something changes in his eyes. "Know her? Had one hell of a crush on her when we were kids. I'm not kidding when I say you're lucky." The onceover he gives me says he doesn't agree with Shannon's decision, but he has no choice.

That's right.

He doesn't.

"You're right about that," is all I say, his jaw tightening.

Andrew stands next to me, his arms crossed over his chest, body leaning just slightly in my direction. Nonverbal communication triggered by his inner caveman is clear:

We can take him.

"We've known Perlman since he and Shannon were preschoolers," Jason explains, with a panoramic gesture that takes in the farm through the thickening snow. "Our family has come here for more than thirty years to get our trees."

Perlman winks at him. "And this year's the big one, isn't it?"

Jason's sly smile makes the back of my neck tingle again.

"Sure is."

"All our trees have done well by you, huh?" Perlman asks, the question making Jason's face fall.

Andrew smirks and I smother a laugh with my hand. Perlman, who's no idiot, is quick to pick up on our reaction.

"They've all been fine," Jason says in an evasive tone that makes Perlman's forehead jump up three inches, the wool cap sliding up with his eyebrows.

"You've never said that about one of ours, Jason! Was something wrong with last year's tree?"

"No, not last year's."

"I wasn't here the last two years. Up in Canada looking at a piece of equipment two years ago, and last year Pops was sick. Danny from Dover filled in. What was wrong? Too old? Too green? Too–"

"Hot," I mutter, which makes Andrew start to laugh uncontrollably.

"Excuse me?"

Jason gives me a pained look, but before I can spill the truth about the flaming Christmas debacle, in which Chuckles the cat and Chuffy the dog somehow managed to set the tree–and part of the Jacoby house–on fire two years ago, a big snowball hits Andrew smack on the cheekbone.

Which makes me laugh.

Hard.

Until I get one to the back of the neck, too.

Multi-octave giggles, the kind that can only come from biological males going through puberty, pierce the air as the wind picks up, whipping snow in my face. A wall of kids points and laughs at us, the mis-named Boomers, and I can feel the atmosphere change.

They've just launched first strikes at the most competitive men in the world.

They do not realize what they have unleashed.

Perlman acts first, dipping like a pro-league fielder to scoop up a handful of snow and wing it at Jeffrey, who takes the hit full on the face, the surprised O of his mouth smashed with snow. It makes Jason laugh, but he gets hit smack in the chest, the white spot on his black parka like a misshapen heart. Ducking, he barely misses a projectile from Jordan, who has one hell of an arm.

Game on, kids.

May the better Boomer win.

Perlman and Jason, Andrew and I turn into partners with flow, nonverbal cues enough to find a steady pace. What the kids might have in energy and enthusiasm, they lack in experience, their sheer volume overwhelmed by our targeted attacks. Tyler lays flat on the ground, staring up into the sky, biting the falling snow like a puppy, arms and legs making a snow angel.

Soon Jordan joins him, the two a giggling mass of kid.

Jeffrey and Steegan, though–those two are future Harvard MBAs. They have strategy, agility, and the drive to win.

Too bad Andrew and I are stronger.

And we don't pander.

"What're you doing?" Jason huffs at us as Andrew lobs a steady stream of snowballs from the supply I'm giving him, my hands going through the motions like we're an assembly line and I'm Henry Ford's test case.

"WINNING!" I shout.

"They're kids! Let them have the honor."

Andrew and I halt dead in our tracks at the words, spoken by a man who is a father figure to us on some level.

"WHAT?" we both shout, shocked by his sacrilege.

This is an error.

A huge one.

Never let yourself be taken off guard by unexpected emotion.

Because it means you *lose*.

Smelling blood, Jeffrey and Steegan adapt our strategy and use it against us. An observant Jordan peels away from Tyler to join the pack, the Zoomers taking on the Millennials while Jason just shakes his head sadly, as if our competitive streak disappoints him.

But Perlman gets it.

The three of us form a wall against the four kids, Jason flanking us, eventually hiding behind a contraption attached to a big roll of plastic mesh that confuses me.

"Don't move the level on the tree wrapper!" Perlman calls out to Jason, just as a huge snowball explodes in a puff of hilarity right on his forehead. Snow coats his moustache and beard like he's Santa.

"What's a tree wrapper?" I ask Andrew as we duck to avoid an onslaught from Steegan, who appears to have grown a second set of arms.

"How would I know? You ever buy your own Christmas tree?"

"Of course not. My assistant always does it."

A huge rush of wind sets the snow blowing sideways, the rate of it increasing suddenly, a brief whiteout squall that ends with my head getting hit from two separate directions. I lock my knees to stay upright, as if that matters somehow, the icy balls knocking straight against my open mouth as surprise turns me into a victim.

"VICTORY IS OURS!" Jordan screams.

"FREEEEEDOMMMMMMM!" The scouts roar in unison, as if any of them have seen a certain movie that came out when I was a child.

You know, me? The alleged Boomer?

As the scouts re-enact *Lord of the Flies*, Jason comes out from behind the big mesh roller and brushes himself off, laughing. Perlman yanks off his wool cap and shakes the chunk of snow off it, while Andrew glowers at the celebrating kids.

"We whipped their asses," he mutters, as if saying it makes it true.

Jeffrey starts hooting.

"WE CREAMED YOU, MUTHAH–"

"SCOUTS!" Jason shouts over his grandson, giving the kid a glare that could peel paint.

Testosterone poisoning is particularly painful to watch in a thirteen-year-old.

But it feels different when they've just whomped us in a competition.

"Let's get those wreaths and the tree," Perlman says to Jason, looking up at the sky. A lazy flake lands on his nose, melting instantly. "I don't like what this storm is up to."

"It's just snow," I say, Perlman coming to a full halt as the words come out of my mouth.

Sniffing the air, he gives me a skeptical look that says I'm a dumbass. "Smell that?"

I flare my nostrils and inhale. "I smell air. Cold air."

"I smell trouble."

"That's vague."

"Snow has a scent. When the flakes are big like this, whiteout is steady, and gusts come along to blow the cold air, it means we may have a nor'easter coming."

Andrew holds up his phone. "Nope. Nothing about that until tomorrow."

"Then we need to get you all out of here. Besides, we've got a Balsam fir to cut."

"A tree?" Andrew clues in quickly. "I thought we were only doing wreaths."

"You didn't tell them?" Perlman goggles at Jason, who goes sheepish and mercenary at the same time.

It's quite a look.

"Tell us what, Jason?" I demand.

"The tree? He hasn't mentioned *the tree*?" Perlman clearly likes sharing a secret with Jason that I know nothing about.

I get Shannon all to myself in bed, so who's got more power, bud?

"Tree?" Andrew asks.

Unable to avoid it any longer, Jason approaches us, one hand on each of our necks, and we huddle like the Pats at fourth down, Bill Belichick glowering.

"I needed chaperones, yes. And I wanted to spend time with

you away from the women. Why not just hang out? Give you a preview of life with older kids?"

"Get to the point," I grind out.

"Jason's been watching this damn tree now for a couple of decades," Perlman explains.

Jason looks like a fish gasping for air.

"A tree?"

"Not just any tree. *The* tree." Jason's reverential hush makes me hold my breath. Plenty of men use that kind of voice for their most prized possessions, including wives, mistresses, cars, rare coins, and signed baseballs from the World Series, but my father-in-law isn't those guys.

"*The* tree?" I repeat.

"The tree. The mother of all trees."

"The mother of all trees," Perlman echoes with a half grin, attention solely on Jason. It's clear the two share a bond, one I am absolutely, positively, not even a *tiny* bit jealous of as the realization of their relationship dawns on me.

"Where is it? Let's bring it back to Mendon and give it the place of honor it deserves," I call out, ready to act.

Ready to be the guy who enables Jason's fantasy.

"You can't, no, Declan, it doesn't work that way," Jason says softly, the look he shares with Perlman making me want to kill the guy. Andrew would grab a shovel and help hide the body, right?

"How does it work?"

"We need to get the wreaths in the van. Then, at the last minute, when the temperature is perfect, we cut that baby down. Perlman uses the mesher on it if it fits, then we tie it to the top of the van. We drop all the scouts off, take the wreaths home, store them in my garage until we're ready for the sale, and we unload this big boy into the house, where Marie will orgasm on the spot from the sheer joy of seeing Bessie in our house."

"Bessie?"

"We named her the day we planted her."

"*Planted* her?" I ignore the orgasm comment. So does Perlman. Andrew is suddenly lobbing snowballs at Tyler, who is playing dodgeball with them.

And winning.

"Yep," Jason says, his gaze unfocused, mind and memory in

the past. "We planted ten trees here when Marie was pregnant with Amy. Seven of them made it. We've cut down and proudly used six of them, the last one about seven years ago, before you and Shannon met, Declan. This is the last one."

"Are you sure you want to cut her down?" I ask.

Nodding, Jason gives me a wistful smile. "I am. Almost cut Bessie down two years ago, but decided to wait. Glad I did."

"She would have burned down," Andrew marvels.

Perlman's eyes widen. "Burned down?"

"Long story," I start to explain, but Jason jumps in.

"Our cat and dog got a little rambunctious and, well... it's complicated."

"I'd love to hear it." His eyes cut to the kids. "Some other time, when you're not hauling young 'uns."

"It's a three-beer story," Jason says with a sigh.

"I'll bet."

"GRANDPA?" Jeffrey shouts. "Can we get the wreaths and go? We all want the hot chocolate at your house when we get back."

Bzzz

Andrew's phone.

"Sorry. Must be Amanda." He pulls his phone out from under layers of ski clothes and frowns. "Yeesh."

"What's wrong?" Jeffrey asks, nosing over Andrew's arm.

Andrew flashes the phone at us. Amanda's sent a picture via text.

"Is that a baby's back?" Jeffrey asks, squinting. "Why is there mustard all over it?"

"Thank God the nanny's here," Andrew reads aloud. *"Charlie and Will are engaged in a poop-off."*

"POOP-OFF!" Tyler screams.

"Ah, geez," Jason says, rubbing his neck in frustration. "That's the last thing we need to hear Tyler repeat all the way home."

Tyler holds his hands up to his mouth and begins making juicy fart noises again.

"Let's get you those wreaths, and Bessie," Perlman says, walking off toward the barn, waving us along. "Come on in. Fire's going and it's warm in here."

Following the smoke, we find ourselves at a sliding barn door that Perlman moves like it's a minor annoyance, but it must weigh three hundred pounds. A blast of warm air, woodsy and instantly relaxing, envelops us.

The kids flock to the heat and stare up at the high-ceilinged barn. It's clean, orderly, and absolutely stuffed with junk.

Neat junk.

"How's the estate going?" Jason asks Perlman as we let the kids encircle the wood stove, Andrew turned away from me, head down.

Texting.

"Fine. You know Pops. Never met a piece of old farm equipment he could turn down."

Jason looks around the three-story barn, broken-down metal machinery everywhere, and lets out a low whistle. "What'll you do with it all?"

"Got some collectors coming. They'll pay a pretty penny for some of these machines from the 1920s and '30s. The rest goes to metals dealers."

"How much you think you've got here?" I ask.

He quotes a number larger than I expect.

"Who is Pops?" I ask, making small talk.

"My grandfather. He died back in March."

"I'm sorry. My condolences."

"He was a hundred and four. Lived a good, long life. Half this stuff he bought new, back in the day, and just hung onto it. Anything gets old enough, it becomes an antique."

"Even people," Jason says with a friendly grin.

Perlman gives him a quiet look and a soft smile. "Yeah, that. Pops lived through so much. Born during WWI. Can you imagine? Didn't have a radio when he was a kid. Got his first television when he was almost fifty. Thought the internet was some kind of joke. The man knew what to do with his mind and his hands combined, though. Don't make 'em like him anymore."

"No. They make them better," Jason says, hand on Perlman's shoulder. "There's more than enough of Pops in you, son."

Jason has a way of making people feel seen. The kids watch the conversation, every single one of them, even if it doesn't seem like it.

And from the hunch of Andrew's shoulders, it's clear he's paying attention, too, thumbs quiet.

"That means a lot to me, Jason." Perlman looks around, head tipped up, eyes cataloguing the barn with a sense of context the rest of us don't have. "So much of this is him. Letting it go feels like letting him go some more, too. But we can't hold onto it all, and we sure could use the money from selling it."

"Business is down?" Jason inquires politely. Out of the corner of my eye, I see Steegan and Jeffrey gently shoving each other, the other scouts beginning to fidget. Warmed up now and partially dried off, they're getting restless.

Based on Andrew's impatient movements as he bends over his phone, they're not the only ones.

"It's farming. Tree farming, no less. Business itself is fine, but all the costs associated with it are up. We're all just one bad disaster away from folding. That derecho storm in Iowa is a reminder of that."

"You think one of those could hit here? In downeast Maine?"

Perlman snorts. "Vermont sure as heck didn't think a hurricane would hit them and remember the one that did back in 2011? Irene?"

Jason groans. "Don't remind me. We lost power for days in Massachusetts and we got off easy."

"Parts of Vermont were demolished. That kind of rain is great when it's spread out over a month or two, not concentrated in a couple of days. Bad flooding like that and we're ruined."

"How'd we get from nostalgia about Pops to being all doom and gloom?" Jason asks, one eye suddenly on Steegan, who is poking the wood stove with a fire iron.

"'Cause we're human and realists," Perlman says, clapping Jason on the back before turning to me and asking, "What kind of business you in?"

"Coffee."

His mouth turns down, eyebrows up. He approves. "Then you know all about how natural disasters affect the crops."

"Right. Good luck getting your hands on anything out of central America right now after that hurricane."

"Friend of mine works with Fair Trade people down in Guatemala. Yep." The change in Perlman's demeanor toward me is palpable. I've gone from suspicious stranger to fellow businessman with something in common.

Something other than being attracted to my wife.

I nudge Andrew, whose elbow is rigid from rapid texting. "Hey. Cut it out. Role model and all that."

He gives me a look that tells me I'm not going to like whatever he's about to say.

"Work problem," he says tersely.

"Not Amanda this time?"

"No. But if I don't get out ahead of a labor mess at one of our properties, I'll pay for it."

"Berlin? Paris? Toronto?"

"Bolton."

"Bolton? Where's that?"

"About forty minutes west of Boston."

"Anterdec has a property there?"

"What? No, not Anterdec. One of the gyms."

I start laughing. Can't help it.

"You're *personally* handling issues at a gym? You can't have more than, what–ten employees?"

"Seven, all of them part time. Someone complained about one of the high schoolers wearing a political slogan on a pin while at work, and now the local Facebook page has erupted into a free for all, complete with boycotts of the chain being promoted in the region."

"Andrew."

"What?"

"Why are you micromanaging this? Hand it off to marketing."

"I *am* marketing."

"What?"

"I am marketing for now. Amanda's busy with the babies. Nannies are taking vacation during the holidays. Haven't had time to hire anyone."

"Gina can't do the marketing hiring for you?"

"Gina is overloaded at Anterdec. Dad's being a jerk."

"That's nothing new."

"He's worse since I quit. Making everything three times harder than it has to be."

"You've hit your wall."

"I have. Yes. The twins are walking and talking up a storm and all I want to do is grow my gyms and hang out at home."

I grab my phone, earning a disapproving look from Jason, and start typing.

"What're you doing?"

"Helping you."

Bzzz

Both our phones light up as my executive assistant, Dave, answers immediately.

What do you need?

Andrew has a local labor problem involving social media. Can't find time to hire a marketing person. Can you help?

I don't work for Anterdec. Too corporate for me. Cutthroat billionaires are the scourge of society.

Andrew looks at me with a *WTF?* expression.

"That's his idea of helping?"

"He's an anarchist with an MBA from Wharton. Dave's nothing but contradictions. You have to know how to play him." I hold up one finger for Andrew to pause, then type:

Andrew's a scourge. I'll give you that.

"HEY!"

The scouts turn in unison to look at us, bent over our phones.

Immediately, they all pull theirs out, earning a groan from Jason.

But the scourge's money could be earned by someone like you who wants to transfer wealth from capitalist hoarders to causes that matter.

"You have got to be kidding me," Andrew mutters, glancing at Jordan. "Are Dave and that kid related?"

Fair point, Dave replies. *I know a marketing expert who could be willing to use her skills for evil for the right price and a hefty corporate donation to Food Not Bombs.*

They wouldn't be working for Anterdec. This is for Andrew's new company. The gyms.

Why didn't you say so?

"You realize I'm on the group text, Declan." Andrew's thumbs start flying.

Bzzz

I don't need an anarchist who will look down on my corporate growth and sabotage my profit margins for the sake of some ideology, he texts to us.

"That's not going to make Dave want to help you."

"Wait and see."

"Reverse psychology doesn't work on him."

"What does?"

"Money."

"How does an anarcho-primitivist justify being motivated by money?"

"How does someone go from a major in folklore to a Wharton MBA to living in a squatter's community, where he makes artisanal chocolate in a bathtub? I don't know. I just know the guy isn't going to appreciate being insulted like that."

No one plans to sabotage anything, Andrew. Give Karla a percentage of all profits directly attributed to marketing and social media efforts and you'll see growth.

Karla? Andrew texts back.

She goes by Karla Marcks.

"Oh, God," Andrew groans. "I am not hiring someone like that. Dad would kill me."

"Dad has nothing to do with your gyms."

His head pulls back in surprise. "Oh. Right."

I clap him on the shoulder. "Took me a while to shake Dad off, too. You'll get there."

Fine, Andrew texts the group chat. *Have Karla send Gina a resume.*

That's not how this works. You have to convince her.

"Since when do I have to sell an employee on the company?" he demands, as if I'm the one who said that.

As we talk, Jason and the scouts file out of the warm barn. We follow them, a burst of chilled air making my face jolt.

"Hey. We need to focus on the here and now."

"I am!" he insists.

"*This* here and now. With the scouts. Remember? We're here to help. Work shouldn't interfere."

"Since when?"

"Since we decided to have more control over our lives."

"I'm building a business, Dec."

"Yes. And Jason's doing something worthwhile, too. He asked us to help."

Andrew adds Gina to the group chat and texts, *Gina, take it from here.*

Dave immediately replies: *I'm already texting with her. You're no longer needed.*

"The balls on that guy," Andrew mutters, which just makes me blink.

A lot.

And change the subject.

The snow has let up, a thick, downy coating of it on the van's front, the back doors open wide. Jason has expertly packed the back row of the van with big white boxes that smell like evergreen, as they should.

"Half the wreaths fit in the back row just fine, and we still have all the cargo space behind that," he explains as the kids walk out like ants moving food to their queen.

"Need help?" Andrew asks, as Jason holds up a hand to stop him.

"Let the kids do it. They need the exertion and to feel the hard work in their bodies."

Andrew and I frown at each other. What the hell does that even mean?

"James taught all three of you the value of hard work, right?" he prods, clearly reading our confusion.

"Sure. But he always told us a smart man uses his mind to make money, and a sucker uses his body," Andrew explains.

"Though when he's had enough whisky, he exempts escorts from that."

The long, disgusted sigh that comes out of Jason makes it clear what he really thinks of Dad.

"I know he's a little older than me and we didn't cross paths, but your father is very familiar with using his hands to make a living. You didn't grow up in the Boston neighborhood we came from and not know how to scrape by with manual labor."

"He's told us stories, but we were never allowed to have jobs anywhere but at Anterdec," I reply, making Jason's eyebrows jump.

"I don't–it never occurred to me that we... could?" Andrew's thought makes his voice rise at the end, as if the question itself is bringing up new territory for him to consider.

"James didn't make you get a summer job?"

"We interned at Anterdec."

"You didn't work a paper route? Babysit? Summer camp

counselor?" He scratches his chin as Perlman waves to him, indicating the last box is held by Jeffrey, who comes to the van and rests it on the bumper. "You started in the mailroom, I hope?"

"My first job was interim assistant director of marketing," I explain. "I was nineteen, summer after my freshman year at Harvard."

"I think mine was interim assistant director of operations," Andrew adds.

"Pretty sure Terry was interim assistant director of finance," I say, trying to remember.

"What a way to earn your first paycheck," Jason says sadly. "You've never had a job where you got to feel in your bones how the rest of us live. There's value in learning how to navigate around asshole bosses."

"Oh, we know that one all too well," Andrew informs him.

"James McCormick has nothing on a shift supervisor at a fast food joint. Or dock foreman at a package handling facility," Jason says with a terseness that reminds me how much money shapes us.

And how I can never understand him through that lens.

"You're right," I say to him, needing to diffuse this tension that isn't productive, though it's important. "We don't know that kind of hustle. We have no idea what it's like to have our next meal or the roof over our head reliant on pleasing a petty tyrant."

He stands down, nodding.

"But we do know about the anger of having unfair expectations set on us, and feeling powerless in the face of a tyrannical boss."

A bleak look fills my brother's eyes.

"Grandpa?" Tyler pulls on Jason's sleeve. "Want to go home now."

Jason startles and looks at the van, where the scouts stand in a semicircle, the task complete.

"Ok, scouts. Great job! How many wreaths do we have?" He looks at Perlman.

"Twenty to a box."

"And how many boxes?" He asks Steegan.

"Seventeen."

"Three hundred and forty wreaths!" Tyler calls out unprompted.

"And how much does each wreath cost?" Jason asks Perlman, though it's clear he already knows the answer. This is part of the lesson for the scouts.

For the next five minutes, Jason does a run-through on cost, price, profit margin, and basic Business 101, while Andrew texts and I ignore him. A leisurely stroll around the driveway shows me that to the right of the barn, a wide road takes you back to an old white farmhouse with black shutters and a wraparound porch, and a chicken coop the size of a three-bay garage. The house has two additions that look like they were built fifty or so years ago, the long, uniform, two-story attachments much newer looking than the old-fashioned New England construction of the main house.

"Like the place?" Perlman asks, suddenly at my side.

"I do. What are the additions?"

"Seasonal farm labor. Back when Pops and my dad had this place really going, we had migrant workers here almost year-round, between the regular crop and the Christmas greenery."

"Those are big additions. How many workers?"

"They house families. Six apartments in all."

"Families?"

"Pops put in the first addition for the men who came in the 1940s, but then those men had wives. Kids. Eventually, Pops realized he'd have a more stable workforce if he offered apartments. We still have four guys from Jamaica who come here every year."

"Are they here now?"

"Two are. They're my dad's age, so they're close to retiring."

"Their kids didn't stay in the business?"

"Their kids were able to get trade and university educations because of their parents' work here. All of them stayed in Jamaica and built their local economy."

"There's a lot more to a small farm in Maine than meets the eye, isn't there?"

"Always more than meets the eye. Always."

"Listen, Perlman," I say, pulling out my wallet. "I want to cover the cost of the wreaths."

"You what?"

"I'll explain it to Jason later. Consider it a donation to the Boy Scouts."

"Afraid I can't let you do that, Declan."

"Why not? Is this about teaching kids lessons on fortitude and strength and doing it on your own?"

"No," he says blandly. "It's because your brother already Venmo'd me the cost of all three hundred forty wreaths."

"He... he..."

A hearty clap on the shoulder, followed by an enormous grin, is Perlman's response.

And then the words, "He beat you to it, huh?"

It's a good thing there isn't a weapon nearby, because I'd beat Andrew with it right now.

Speaking of which, at that moment, a tap on my shoulder makes me whirl around to find Jason standing there, ax in hand.

"It's time," he says to Perlman, voice grave and deep, as if he's about to execute a convicted criminal.

Or put an animal out of its misery.

Perlman nods, leading us down a long row of trees, cutting right, then left, then right, until we're at the edge. Andrew's behind me, followed by a line of ducklings in scout form.

We turn, a wide expanse with a single fat tree before us.

"I assume this is Bessie?"

Wordless wonder covers Jason's face, to the point of tears.

No, really. I swear the man is crying over the bliss of a tree. He looks at that Balsam fir the way my father looks at the new crop of female interns every June at Anterdec.

"She's ready. Pops said so the last couple of years, but you waited."

"Glad I did. It was bad enough losing Pops this year. If we'd lost Bessie to a stupid fire caused by a deranged cat and a clueless dog, I couldn't have looked you in the face with any dignity."

Says the man who pees in a coffee can in his man cave.

"Say what?"

"I told you it's a three-beer story," Jason says with a hearty laugh that makes Perlman's eyes light up.

"You'll have to come back and tell me that one." His eyes cut to the scouts. "Some time when you're not in charge of all these kids."

Jason stares at Bessie and nods, mind already a million miles away.

Lust reveals itself in radically different ways in men. For most, the baser instincts drive the emotion, all of them rooted in their, well...

Root.

For others, it's a lust for money. Or power.

For Jason, it's this tree.

A damn *tree.*

Over the years, I've been in plenty of negotiations, in boardrooms, at bars, in fine dining establishments, on yachts. I've made counter-offers on golf courses, in hot tubs, poolside, and on motorbike trails.

And in every single instance, there's a point where you see the lust to acquire in the eyes of the other person, knowing full well you're revealing your own to them.

Jason has never shown this side of himself to me before.

Then again, I've never spent this kind of time with him, been able to observe him in a holy moment.

"You sure about this?" Perlman asks, tapping Jason's arm that holds the ax.

"As sure as anything in my life. Bessie is mine," he growls. "She's coming home."

My spine straightens as if called to war by my chieftain. Even Andrew feels it, the scouts going to a hushed quiet, the snow seeming to part as we stare at the lush wonderland of Bessie's fat middle. She's symmetrical, conical in a perfect ratio, green and mossy like my eye color. The frosted hint at her branch tips creates a nuanced, sophisticated look.

"Scouts," Jason calls out in a sure, confident voice. "This is the best Christmas tree you'll ever lay eyes on."

"Because it's not on fire," Jeffrey says slowly, earning giggles from his friends and a cold, steely look that turns Jason from affable grandpa to cruel warlord.

The click from Jeffrey's throat as he swallows sounds like an ax chop.

"Grandpa?" Tyler asks softly, standing next to Andrew and reaching for my brother's hand. The movement surprises Andrew but he earns a hat tip for smoothly accepting my nephew's gesture, understanding intuitively that even the kids realize this isn't the Jason they usually know before us.

Tyler's soft inquiry seems to shake Jason from his obsessive state. "Yes?"

"The tree is fat."

"Yes, it is."

"Too big."

"It's too big?"

Wide-eyed, Tyler nods his head.

"Will it fit in the living room?" Jason asks.

Tyler shakes his head.

"Do you think Grandma will like it?"

"Grandma likes everything."

Jason beams at him. "She sure does."

"Grandma likes secret cake."

"Secret cake?"

"It's not a secret if you tell everyone, Tyler!" Jeffrey informs him, making the other scouts snicker.

"Secret means you don't tell!" Tyler announces, beaming.

Marie's been busted. Secret cake, indeed. Now I'm wondering what bakery delights my own wife is hiding from me. She learned from a master, clearly.

"Bessie is the crowning glory of years of work and patience. We planted her with nine other saplings more than twenty-eight years ago, and now here we are." Is that a tear in the corner of Jason's eye?

"Amy's twenty-eight?" I ask Andrew, who shrugs.

"How the hell would I know?"

Marching to the fat fir, which is enormous – a good forty feet tall – Jason strokes her outer branches like a lover he's seeing for the first time after years of separation. His touch is so intimate, I want to look away. This feels private, raw, and vulnerable, and I'm instantly embarrassed for my father-in-law.

Meanwhile, Andrew takes pictures.

"What are you doing?"

"Jason looks like he's about to hump that tree," he says out of the corner of his mouth.

"Andrew!"

"What? He does. Who knew a man could be so besotted with a *tree?*"

"You're that way about collecting *Yes* albums."

"Am not!"

"Are, too. We all have our thing."

"But a tree, Dec? Is this really why we're here? To help him with that damn beast?"

It dawns on me that Andrew's right. We're here because Jason needs help. We're accessories to a tree's death for the sake of Jason's obsession. If he's Ahab and Bessie is his Moby Dick, we're the spears.

The rumble of an old truck's engine cuts through the air as Andrew's question rings in my ears. Perlman pulls up in a Ford that has to be as old as he is and rolls the window down.

Actually rolls it down, with a crank.

"Hey, all. Gotta go. Pellet shipment for the wood stove came in at the lumberyard and I need to get my bulk order, then I'm headed up to Fryeburg for a bowling tournament and staying overnight with a friend. Jason, you can take it from here?"

Jason nods and looks at me and Andrew. "Sure can. I've got good help."

Andrew's jaw clenches as I come to the same realization.

We're labor.

Nothing but *labor*.

Jason may have wanted us here for male bonding or fatherly crap with the kids, but he also has an agenda.

An unarticulated one.

And he's not above manipulating us to accomplish his goals.

"Why couldn't he just have Perlman help him cut down the tree? Why the subterfuge?" Andrew asks as we hold our ground and don't follow Jason to Bessie.

"No idea."

THWACK.

We turn and look to see Jason take the first chop.

"Is he actually crying?" Andrew asks.

"Is Mr. Jacoby okay?" Jordan whispers, looking to me as if I have the answer.

Oh. Right. We're the adults.

"It's like he's putting down an injured animal," Steegan says. "My dad bagged a ten-point buck once and he cried. He wasn't sad, he said. Just emotional."

"No. It's more like how you feel after years of putting

together the perfect deal," I try to explain. The kids give me confused looks. "Or, um, a science fair project. All that work pays off, finally."

"Like building a robot for robotics team!" Jordan pipes up, understanding dawning in their eyes. "You solder electronics all day, and all the next day, and then there's that moment of triumph when your robot finally chases the cat across the kitchen floor!"

"Exactly," I reply, not sure it's really an exact comparison, but close enough.

Each strike of the ax is precise, Jason's blows strong and sure. Most people would use a chainsaw, but there's an artisanal elegance to his motion. He's doing this, man vs. nature, man with nature, and I feel like we're part of some ancient ritual, as if sap and blood once ran together through our veins.

And then:

"Declan!"

I hear the call of my clan leader.

Careful not to break or bend Bessie's branches, I step into her, reaching for the trunk at mid-height, holding her steady. Andrew stands with the kids, uncertain yet transfixed. Never in our lives has our own father asked us to partake in any activity like this.

Not only are we doing something outdoors with our hands, we're being invited into the emotion of it.

We're on another planet here.

"Andrew!" Jason calls out as Bessie leans, one more final, tender blow enough to detach her from her root ball and bring her out of the earth, to be reborn and brought to her final home in Mendon. Heeding the call, Andrew comes to us and, as Jason's final *thwack* completes a twenty-eight-year plan, we let her rest gently on the ground.

Because there's no way that huge tree is making it to Mendon as is.

"I have to top her off," he announces, going to a spot on the trunk where he'll cut the top thirteen or fifteen feet or so. It seems like a waste, but we watch, hypnotized, as he makes the perfect cut with a surgeon's precision, then shears the lower branches off, leaving a Christmas tree of evergreen and a thirty-foot log, which he cuts in half.

"There. Marie can take the branches and make wreaths from them. Mantel decorations. Centerpieces," he says solemnly, pointing to the tree.

We lift her up and onto our shoulders, like pallbearers carrying a great burden.

And an even greater honor.

"Why is everyone so serious?" Steegan whispers, which makes something gleam in Jeffrey's eye. I'm long past him, ten feet from the van, when the inevitable happens.

THWACK!

This one isn't the strike of an ax.

It's the impact of a snowball at the base of my neck.

The little stinkers realize they have us at their mercy, and we're targets.

"Jerks," Andrew mutters, except the word he says isn't *jerks*, and they hear it, laughing their butts off as we get hit over and over. No one aims for Jason, who is holding the base and grinning like a kid on a bike running downhill, feet splayed off the pedals, wind whipping him into another time.

The mesher is too small for this one, so Jason ties her up lovingly like a dom with a rope fetish. She's way easier to handle that way.

And now I'm anthropomorphizing a tree.

We get to the van and Jason calls out, "On the count of three, lift. One, two, three!"

As we lift, Tyler throws a snowball and hits my armpit dead on.

Once the tree is on the van's roof, I turn and tackle him, his giggles making me stand down and laugh with him, my pretending to smush his face in the snow triggering a mix of laughter and fear in him that shows itself in waves. Tyler's an odd little beast, but a sweet one.

Some people in this world don't fit into boxes as easily as others. Tyler is one of them.

"SCOUTS!" Jason shouts, as if coming out of a trance and realizing what's happening. "We need to tie the tree on the roof and get going. Jeffrey, you go and collect all the tree branches I sheared off and put them in the black trash bags in the back of the van."

"Why are we getting a tree, Mr. Jacoby?" Jordan asks, snow

sticking to their long, blond hair. "I thought this was a wreath sale?"

"It's my tree, Jordan. I planted it here, twenty-eight years ago. Now she's nice and ready."

"Ready to be killed," Jordan says. "You planted new ones, right? To keep the carbon dioxide balance and offset carbon issues?"

"This kid is going to end up being one of those protestors who lives in a tree and pees in a bucket," Andrew says out of the side of his mouth.

"It balances out. Jeffrey's a future hedge fund manager."

Jason secures the ropes on the tree, triple checking all around.

"What about the mesher, Grandpa?" Jeffrey asks, pointing to the machine.

"I think we're fine without it. Pretty sure it's so big, it won't fit anyhow. I roped her off."

Andrew snickers. Jeffrey picks up on it, a strange sort of shock flitting through his eyes, as if grown-ups didn't turn innocent phrases into vulgar innuendo.

Hey, kid. Who do you think started it all?

"Pile in! Time to head back home. All aboard the Mendon Express!" He looks at me and Andrew. "By way of Boston and Weston, of course."

"Can you just drop me off at the Portland airport?" Andrew says, clearing his throat after that. It's one of the rare times I've ever detected guilt in my brother, and it makes me groan inside, already upset by whatever he's up to.

"Airport?" All of us, including every scout except Tyler, say the word in unison, surprised.

Sheepishness doesn't wear well on Andrew, but cold command sure does.

"I am still the CEO of a Fortune 500 company, and there's another crisis. I was able to be here for most of this, and it was fun," he adds, voice softening at the end, dropping so only Jason and I can hear. "But I have to catch a flight, and we drive right past the Portland airport. It saves you the trip to Weston."

Disappointment floods me. It shouldn't but it does.

Is this how Shannon feels when I push family life aside for work?

"It's fine," Jason says, rallying as the scouts all climb into the van, arguing about who sits where in the newly organized space, the back row cut off by wreaths. "And no problem. Of course, we can take you there. I'm sure whatever's going on is important."

Andrew's brow drops. He's reading Jason. The same sentence–*I'm sure whatever's going on is important*–from Dad's mouth would be a barb.

From Jason, it's sincere.

Andrew takes the spot in the first row, while I take shotgun next to Jason.

"Scouts buckled?" Jason calls back.

"BUCKLED!"

"Adults ready?"

"MORE THAN READY!" Andrew booms.

"Alrighty then," Jason says, grinning like a fiend. "Here we go, home for the great unveiling."

He turns the key in the ignition.

And nothing happens.

Turns it again.

Click

7

Shannon

IF THERE IS ONE THING YOU NEED TO KNOW ABOUT MY mother, it's this: She's generous with advice, information, and product recommendations. Especially the advice.

But she's stingy as can be when it comes to her Yankee Swap secrets.

Until my cat and her dog nearly burned the house down on Christmas, the annual Yankee Swap was Mom's time to shine. A weird tradition in its own right, it tends to be the province of weirdos. I mean, who came up with the idea to bring the craziest gift possible, have people pick numbers out of a hat, and then systematically steal the most prized gift from each other?

You have to have a sense of humor *and* be a bit of a sadist–and a holiday one at that–to enjoy such a ritual.

And "funny eclectic sadist" has my mother written *allll* over it.

While Declan is up north with Dad, Tyler, Jeffrey, and Andrew, getting wreaths and finding his special tree, I left Ellie with our nanny, Mia, for a day of shopping with Mom. Being married to a billionaire has its financial perks, so you'd think we'd spend the day on Newbury Street, but no.

We're at a recycling center in Framingham, staring at a tangled ball of rescued Christmas lights. It's so big that it looks like a mutant cat from outer space hacked it up as a giant plastic green hairball.

We're in the back of this huge warehouse, a place open to the public, part of an enormous complex. *Junkyard* isn't the right term for how Funicularelli's Salvage Yard works. You can dump your junk off here for a fee, or bring working, usable items and drop them off for free. Whatever they can sell, they do, placing it all in a huge showroom floor-like space, where nothing has a price on it.

That's right.

You haggle.

See that gleam in Mom's eye? Her middle name is Haggle.

Marie Haggle Scarlotta Jacoby is in her element.

"Mom?" I call out. Apparently, I've lost her in the lawn chair aisle, where a mountain of cheap plastic chaises have folded themselves into an organized favela, complete with union reps and a water filtration plant. No joke: The pile of chairs is at least two stories high.

"I'm over here!" A hand appears above a rattan curio cabinet that looks like something out of the TV set for *Three's Company*.

"What're you doing?" She's bent over, on her belly, rolling on what looks like a giant barrel on its side, with plastic spikes poking out of it.

"Remember these? Cellulite Buster!" She sings a jingle no self-respecting advertising person would write, but the kind that haunts their nightmares. Rolling onto her back, she sits up, rocking forward, pushing her ample tushie into the spikes. "Mmmmm," she moans. "My glutes are killing me after Jason woke me up this morning for some nookie."

"MOM!"

She scoffs, closing her eyes, rocking to some 1970s disco song she begins to hum. "Oh, please. As if you and Declan didn't get it on. When they have to get up at 4 a.m. for something, the morning wood must be appeased, especially if they're not headed to work with their brains full of job stuff."

I start to argue but snap my mouth shut.

Because she's not wrong.

And now I feel guilty it didn't happen this morning.

"You are three seconds away from a public indecency charge on that thing, Mom."

"Give me five and I'll have an experience even better than the one your father gave me this morning."

I press the ball of my foot against the roller and shove hard enough to make her stand quickly, forced to use her yoga-teacher reflexes. I used to wonder how old Agnes could be so crude. What could make an elderly lady have such a dirty mind?

Now I know.

Dirty old ladies don't *become* that way. They just *are*.

"I am not leaving Ellie with a nanny all day just for you to embarrass me nonstop in public."

Confusion fills her eyes. "Then why did you come shopping with me?"

A bald dude wearing a dirty blue t-shirt with the salvage yard's logo–a dumpster with a heart on it and the words *We Rescue the Junk in Your Trunk!*–passes us, pushing a huge cart loaded with bags of what appear to be stuffed animals. One wheel on the cart gyrates like a dying fish on the beach.

"Ooo, is there a Mickey Mouse in there?" Mom asks.

"You always told me used stuffed animals are nothing but vectors for lice."

"That's true for everything but Yankee Swap."

"You'd give away lice-infested toys?"

"If it's goofy enough to be the most popular item, yes."

"Minnie Mouse," the workman mutters.

"Excuse me?"

"Not Goofy. Minnie Mouse."

Squeak. Squeak. Squeak.

Mom watches as he passes us and begins unloading bag after bag of stuffed animals. I'm starting to feel like we've been teleported to the horror movie version of Al's Toy Barn.

Something hot pink catches my eye, the big swath of color standing out in the dreary grey of fluorescent light hell. As I focus on it, I realize it's a Lisa Frank area rug.

And it's a unicorn.

"I think Carol had that when she was in middle school!" Mom gasps, the sound of my sister's name transporting me instantly back to the mid-1990s, when I was the annoying little sister and Carol saved up all her mother's helper babysitting money to buy that damn rug.

"Did she donate it?" Mendon is close enough to Framingham for this to be possible.

"Oh, no! We still have it."

"You do? In her old room?"

"Probably? It's not on the floor. Maybe in the closet, or in the attic? I was saving it for my granddaughter."

"That's really gendered of you, Mom. What if Jeffrey or Tyler wanted it?"

"I already offered. I'm not that out of touch, Shannon," she says tightly. "I may be at the tail end of the baby boomers, but I'm plenty hip."

"Right, Mom."

"Oh, look! Macrame plant hangers!"

And she's off.

I take a deep breath, filling my lungs with the odors of old wood, various fabric softeners and upholstery cleaners, dried bleach from the recently washed linoleum, and the unique scent every thrift shop has–distinct yet similar. No retail shop with shiny new merchandise from China or Pakistan or Made in the USA can compete with the eclectic beauty of second-hand stores.

Because places like this are repositories of memory and function.

Other people's memories, and the persistence of value.

No one wants to throw away something that's "perfectly good," even if it's scratched a little, has some threadbare spots, or looks a wee bit shabby. We're all the Velveteen Rabbit at some point in our lives, right? Except we go through cycles of rebirth and reinvention, within our own lifespans.

Sometimes the piece of you on display is in need of replacement, other times it's new, and sometimes you just need to find the right person to see you still have value, even if you're a bit used up.

The soft spot in Mom's heart for second-hand stuff came after the very gritty financial need to save money, but it's not a distant second in her reasons for shopping this way. Drawn to the different, the motley, the hidden and buried treasure, she unearths what touches her.

As for why it resonates, who knows?

And, really, who cares? It just does.

That's more than enough.

Once I married Declan, I teleported to a financial dimension that might as well be science fiction for the vast majority of people. Dec considers places like this to be literal trash heaps. When we first met, he thought a thrift shop was an antique shop. After I explained the difference, he was perplexed by the idea that you would buy someone's used items.

He once compared it to buying used condoms or tampons and got an earful from Mom. I've never seen him shut up so fast.

Screech, screech, screech.

Someone's pushing a shopping cart down an aisle on the other side of the enormous warehouse, another cart with a broken wheel. When you spend enough time in discount and secondhand shops, you know that sound all too well. Everything is thrifty in a place like this, even their own equipment.

"Honey! Look! A wine refrigerator!" Mom shouts, her voice echoing. There are only three or four other people in the entire store. Mom's a pro like that, too: She only shops during the quiet times, and she knows when they are. When eBay became a thing, people who make a living buying low and selling high began flocking to places like this, coming during sale days and red-tag clearances to make a small profit off whatever they could find.

Mom avoids those times.

She's not here to make money.

She's here to make *discoveries*.

"A wine refrigerator? Here?" As I turn the corner and follow her gaze, I realize she's staring at a small fridge, the size you use in a dorm room. It has a clear glass front, but it looks... off.

A hospital sticker is on the front, and a big orange warning label with details on how to discard sharps.

"See! You billionaires aren't the only ones who can have these fancy things." Bending into a squat, she starts to lift it.

"What're you doing?"

"Buying it!"

"Mom! I don't think that's a wine refrigerator. I think that's for storing insulin safely!"

"Even better. It'll do double duty if anyone in the family ever develops diabetes."

"Why don't you just store wine in the regular kitchen fridge?"

"Why do wealthy people have wine fridges?"

"So they can have temperature-controlled storage," I say automatically, a mental image of ours flitting through my mind. "But you don't have a collection."

"Not yet," she sniffs. "We haven't been able to have one because we didn't have a wine fridge, silly!"

The guy in the blue t-shirt walks by carrying a big stack of plastic storage bins, three on top of each other, and plunks them down a few feet to Mom's right.

"Excuse me?" she asks him. He's shaved bald, has a greying goatee, and lashless brown eyes that look like a serial killer's.

Until he smiles.

"Yeah? Whatcha need?"

"How much for this?"

He blinks rapidly. "Just that? You're not getting more? Normally, you fill the cart up and we give you a price."

I look at him. "She comes in here that often?"

The guy laughs. "She comes in here so often, we're close to creating one of those punch card systems. You know, buy nine cartloads, get the tenth half off."

"FREE!" Mom exclaims. "It should be free!"

Tension that used to live between my shoulder blades, a muscle memory of a time when money was what I thought about, talked about, worried about, and always needed more of, returns for a brief moment, just long enough for me to realize what I've lost–and gained–over the years.

I didn't marry Declan for his money.

But it sure is true that while money can't buy happiness, it can buy a kind of peace that I deeply appreciate.

As Mom and the guy talk about the fridge, he explains that it's from a lab that studied stool samples.

My brain grinds to a screeching halt.

"Stool? As in poop?" Mom asks, pulling away from her find.

"Yeah. Gotta tell you, it's one of the weirdest junk hauls we ever got. Twenty-five of those. Turns out the government changed some regulation and the lab had to get new ones. Decommissioned these. This is the last one."

"Did you tell everyone what they used to store?"

"Sure. No one cares, right? Just bleach the hell out of it before you put your beer or whatever in. You want it? I'll put it aside for you so you don't have to push it around in the cart."

Mom eyes the fridge, her lips twisted to one side, teeth biting down as she contemplates.

"How much are they going for?" I ask, certain they'll cost more than Mom would ever pay.

"Twenty bucks or so. Depends. You know how it works," he says to Mom. "Fill the cart and we start the fun."

"Fun?" I ask.

"You pay by the cart here."

"There's a flat rate?"

"No. You fill it up, I eyeball it, and give you a price."

"And then I counter with a fairer price."

"Hey, lady. Fair is in the eye of the beholder." He winks at Mom.

"So is value," Mom shoots back.

"Hey! Cory! Getcher ass out on the loading dock!" someone shouts from behind a cheap plastic bi-fold door. Fluorescent lights flicker from what looks like a hallway.

He thumbs toward the voice. "Gotta go. It's the beginning of the month and that means cleanouts."

"Cleanouts?"

"Apartments. People moving. They leave their junk and our guys go and get it." He rubs his palms together in a gesture of eagerness. "Lots of work right now."

"Anything good coming in?" Mom asks breathlessly.

He laughs as he leaves. "You one of those people who think all the good stuff is in the back?"

And then the doors swallow him.

Mom plants her hands on her hips and mutters, "He didn't answer my question."

Cory jogs back, slaps a Reserved sticker on the fridge, and winks at Mom again before rushing away.

"Let's get back to our real goal, Mom."

"We have a goal?"

"The Yankee Swap? Remember?"

"Oh. Right." Funicularelli's uses the same furniture they're selling to display many of their wares. Bookshelves have books on them. Curio cabinets are filled with tchotchkes. If you want to buy the furniture, I assume they clear it and just relocate all the merchandise somewhere else.

I come upon Mom opening and closing a box. Inside is a figure of a woman on her knees, in front of a man with a huge penis.

"MOM!"

"What? It's in a tasteful box."

"What *is* that?" I pick it up and turn it over. "Envelope licker?"

Understanding brightens her eyes. "Oh! I see. Like the little sponges you use when you're a secretary. I wondered why her tongue was so huge."

"What's the point of the guy's... you know?"

"I think you rest the flap of the envelope between his legs and his doinker pushes it close to her sponge tongue."

"DOINKER?" I erupt into uncontrollable giggles. Haven't heard that term before.

"We're opening and closing an office supply item that has a man's raging hard-on as a working part, Shannon, and *doinker* is what makes you fall apart? Really? I raised you better."

"What does raising me have to do with anything?" I ask as Mom quietly closes the box and slips it into the cart.

"Hmph."

"You're actually buying that thing? Is that it? You found your Yankee Swap gift?"

"That? You think *that* would win the Yankee Swap? Heck, no. I'll give that to Agnes."

"Agnes?" I snort. "I'll bet she hand carved that thing seventy years ago."

"Pretty sure she was around when that sponge was born, deep in the ocean."

For the next half hour, we wander, my mind attaching prices to everything. Declan would consider this a gigantic waste of time, insisting that my new assistant, Shayla, could order whatever I need and have it shipped to our house. He's pushing me lately to rely on other people so that I have more time for family life and, to his credit, he's doing the same.

Declan's presence is precious, and we're gradually getting more and more of it.

But farming out the pieces of life that I actually enjoy doesn't make sense to me.

Sure, I could skip all this. Go on eBay and find a quirky item. Order it and help someone to make a tiny profit off the very activity I'm enjoying with Mom right now. Calculating the value of my time and delegating work to people whose time is "worth" less might make sense in a business setting, but these hours with Mom can't be project managed.

My mommy brain downshifts and I start to really enjoy the slow shop. You know the kind, when you take your time, look at everything, reflect on whether you like it, and move on.

So simple.

So rare when you're parenting a little one. How do I prioritize something that's solely for me?

Maybe that's Declan's point. Give over the work that isn't central to who I am, so I can focus on me.

"Shannon?" I turn to find Mom standing there, cart overflowing, holding a ThighMaster.

"Hmm?"

"Which color ThighMaster do you think Jason would like most?"

"Does Dad... have a favorite ThighMaster color?"

"He broke the last one. It was blue."

Do not ask Mom how he broke the ThighMaster. Do not ask Mom how he broke the ThighMaster. Do not ask Mom how he broke the ThighMaster. Do not ask Mom how he broke the–

"He broke it during a Boy Scout meeting."

Whew.

"What was Dad doing with one of those at a Boy Scout meeting?"

"Something to do with teaching the boys how to build a trebuchet. You know. A catapult."

"I know what a trebuchet is. We never learned anything like that in Girl Scouts."

"Maybe Ellie will." She contemplates the item in her hand. "I think I'll get him two. One blue, one pink. Jason said they have a nonbinary child in the troop, so let's get some welcoming colors."

"Why not get green and yellow, then? Just avoid the gender stereotyping entirely."

"Ooo! I like that idea!" Mom pushes her cart down the aisle toward a tangled heap of ThighMasters at least six feet high. "You know," she says, manhandling one, "Jason could attach this to the porch ceiling and it would make a fine plant hanger."

That's what's so great about thrift shopping: You can use your imagination to turn a cheesy '70s "As Seen on TV" product into a functional piece of home décor.

My stomach is now growling so much, it's howling at the moon. We wheel the basket over to Cory, who is chatting with a fellow worker in rapid-fire Portuguese. They finish quickly, and he turns to us.

Mom's entire demeanor changes.

Marie Scarlotta Jacoby has spent her entire life squeezing every bit of value out of every penny she can get her hands on. Declan and I have tried over the years to let our money be theirs, but Dad and Mom are proud to a fault, and it's trickled down to my sister Carol, too. She'll let us help with Tyler's therapies, and we created accounts to fully fund college for both kids, but other than working for Anterdec, she won't take more help.

So we have to get creative.

No, I won't step in and buy this for Mom, though it's tempting. I could hand Cory a couple of hundreds and make his day, but that would strip the thrill of the shop away from Mom. What might seem like kindness and generosity on the face of it really wouldn't be.

But I'm totally buying lunch, and she doesn't get to skimp.

The music to *High Noon* plays in my head, Dad's old westerns with the whistling twang running through as Cory takes a pencil and taps once on every single item in the cart, keeping a mental tally in his head. You can see the adding machine ticking through numbers in his brain, until finally he looks up, moves his mouth soundlessly, then looks at Mom and says, "One seventy-two."

"One twenty-five."

"You're killing me, lady."

"That's not a *no*."

"One sixty."

"*Pffft*. One thirty."

Bzzz

My phone rescues me from their haggle, Declan's text coming at the perfect moment.

How's it going at the dump? he asks.

It's not a dump, and Mom found a new ThighMaster for Dad.

I don't even want to know what that means. Are you having fun?

Yes.

That's what I want to hear.

How's the wreath trip?

Good. You never told me about Perlman.

My heart leaps, galloping in my chest. Oh, dear. He's right. I never did tell him about Perlman.

Is he there? Tell him I said hi.

He's here. And he certainly remembers you.

Texts can't communicate tone or attitude, but Declan's use of the word *certainly* communicates plenty. My husband can be deeply jealous, and this is one of those times when I need to defuse it.

But it's Perlman, for goodness sake! Derpy Perlman. He was a sweet, nerdy kid who had a crush on me forever. Every year from the time I was eleven and he was thirteen, we'd go to get the tree from Pops and Nanny's tree farm and he'd be there, moon-eyed and so besotted with me, I didn't know what to do.

Carol teased me mercilessly the entire car trip home the first year.

And the whole way up *and* back after that.

Perlman was always a gentleman, and never tried anything. Never touched me, never tried to kiss me, nothing.

Maybe if he'd tried, I'd have tried right back. While he was never my type, his crush was sweet, and I had enough awkward years as a teen that it might have been nice to have a stolen kiss from a boy who lived in Maine.

Who am I kidding?

My awkward years weren't limited to my adolescence.

Shannon? Declan texts.

Perlman's an old friend. Stop it.

Best to cut Declan's macho b.s. off at the knees.

Stop what? Just letting you know your old friend thinks I'm lucky for marrying you.

Awwww. That's sweet. Give Perlman a kiss for me, I text back.

Ring!

Mom and Cory, mid-negotiation, both jump at the sound of my phone ringing. Mom's head tilts in inquiry.

"It's Declan. He met Perlman and he's jealous," I explain to her.

"Jealous? Of PERLMAN?"

I shrug. "The man gets jealous when I have a male salesclerk at the shoe store." I open the call.

"That's not funny," Declan snaps.

"I thought it was."

"Perlman loved the kiss, though. Said I used just the right amount of tongue."

"Dec!"

"You didn't tell me about Bessie, either."

"The tree? Dad's cutting old Bessie down this year?"

Mom's in the middle of peeling off the exact amount of cash needed to buy the cart full of stuff when I hear her say, "Can you believe it, Shannon? Finally."

"I haven't been to the tree farm in years, Dec. I hope you're having fun."

"We should bring Ellie up here next year. Start buying our trees here."

"You just want to show Perlman that you own me."

"You're not wrong," he growls. "But they do have nice trees up here, and it's very New England."

"Too bad you never met Pops. He was the Yankee-est Yankee you could ever imagine."

"Jason holds him in high esteem."

"We all did." I pause. "How's Andrew handling the trip?"

"He's been bent over his phone most of the time."

I hear Andrew shout loudly in protest in the background.

"Look, we have to go. I'm calling because there's a gli–"

And he disappears into thin air, the three beeps of the call dropping making me look at my phone as if it's responsible.

"That's weird," I mutter. Declan's phone must have died. Hah! For once, I can tease *him* about not keeping it charged.

"Everything ok?"

"I hope so."

8

Declan

"Damn it." I stare at my phone, trying to figure out a solution. Dave always makes sure I have plenty of external battery devices on me when I travel or have Boston meetings, but I'm on my own time here, and Shannon's about as careful with charging devices as she is with not eating an entire pint of ice cream in one sitting.

"Phone died? We can use mine," Jason says, pulling his out, then frowning. "No signal."

"Duh, Mr. Jacoby. No one has a signal here," Steegan calls out.

"Then what have you been doing on your phones?"

"Playing app-based games."

"Andrew has a signal," Jason says, twisting from the driver's seat toward him. "Let's use your phone."

Andrew frowns. "The van's dead?"

Jason turns the key again.

Click

"Yep."

"Can Perlman give us a jump?" Jeffrey asks.

"He just left."

"Anyone else here?" Jeffrey persists.

"Nope. Besides, we don't know if it's the battery. Could be something else. What we need is Perlman, here."

"When's he getting back?"

"Tomorrow. Remember?" Jason squints, looking out the window, throat moving as he swallows. Being stranded in Maine with a van full of kids and wreaths was not part of the plan.

"I have a solution," Andrew says slowly, typing like mad on his phone. He looks around the van, pointing at each person, counting. "Seven."

"Seven people," Tyler repeats.

"Okay. We can do it," Andrew mutters as he texts someone. With a flourish, he sends the text and announces, "Help is on the way."

"What do you mean?" I ask, but he ignores me, climbing out of the van and walking toward the tree farm.

"Any open fields here?" he asks, walking fast to the right, then cantering around the barn.

"TO THE LEFT!" Jason shouts. "The hay fields?"

I throw his puzzled look at me right back.

"What's he up to?" I mutter, climbing out of the van.

"Mr. Jacoby? My mom and dad will really worry if I don't text them in the next hour. I'm supposed to check in," Jordan explains.

"It's okay. Mr. McCormick has a phone that can text. What's your mom or dad's number?" He opens the glove box and pulls out a pen, turning his wrist over to write on his skin.

Jordan recites the numbers and Jason records them. He climbs out, and I join him on Andrew's heels.

"Andrew! One of the kids needs you to call their parents."

"My phone function isn't working, but text is."

"Great. Let's text Jordan's parents, then text Shannon and Marie and let them know what's going on. We're going to need a rescue, and it's a two-hour drive for Marie. We'll need two cars for all the kids." He looks back longingly at the van. "And the tree."

"The tree?"

"Uh, the tree and the wreaths."

Andrew reads the number on Jason's arm and takes care of the text to Jordan's parents, then texts twice more. I assume he got Shannon and Marie. "Got it all covered."

"Good."

"No, I mean," he says, pointing to the large field, "I've got it all covered. I re-routed the helicopter from Portland Airport to this field. Gave the pilot the address, and he knows the coordinates."

"HELICOPTER?" Jason booms.

"Right. Eight-seater."

"You... you have a helicopter coming right now? A *helicopter?*"

"That's why I needed the ride to Portland Airport."

"To catch a *helicopter?*"

"Sure. Back to Boston."

"I thought you were flying somewhere."

"I am."

"You realize you won't be able to do this much longer," I tell him, though I'm secretly jealous. "Anterdec is yours for only a little while longer."

Andrew winks at me. "All the more reason to milk it while I can."

I turn to Jason. "Don't you have some kind of roadside assistance for the van? Which rental agency did you use?"

"I didn't. It's a friend's van. He lent it to me for free."

This is one part of Jason and Marie's existence I'll never understand. Everyone borrows each other's stuff to get jobs done. Why not rent it under a protection plan? Or hire someone to do it for you?

"Does he need it?"

"He does by Monday. I can ask Perlman for the name of a local auto shop. He'll know someone who can come out and fix it, then Marie and I can come back tomorrow. Worst case, I'll lend him my minivan for a few days." Jason looks embarrassed, as if projecting himself into a future conversation with his friend.

"I can send a mechanic up," Andrew says. "Easy to do." He starts texting.

Jason puts his hand on Andrew's wrist. "That's not how we do things."

"I can tell. The way you do things results in a group of Boy

Scouts being stranded two hours from home. My way gets everyone where they need to be and what they need to function."

Anger isn't a common emotion in my father-in-law. Seeing it on his face, aimed at my brother, catches me off guard.

"That's a really crappy way to throw your money around. Most of us have to solve our own problems."

"I'm not most people."

Before Jason can respond, the thick sound of helicopter blades cuts through the air, scouts turning their faces up to the sky in wonder. Andrew's treatment of Jason can't go unanswered, but I'm torn.

Because they're both right.

"We're flying in *that?*" Steegan shouts with a *yippee,* face lighting up, every element of boy delight flooding his early-teen features.

"I don't know if the permission slip my parents signed covers this, Mr. Jacoby," Jordan says seriously, eyeing the helicopter like it's a dangerous amusement park ride.

"We can be in Boston in less than an hour. And I have a driver with a 14-passenger van in Boston, ready to go," Andrew informs us.

"Why can't they just drive up here and get us?" Jason asks him.

Andrew grins. "Because it wouldn't be as cool as this."

Jason grits his teeth as Andrew helps the kids climb into the helicopter. I expect him to move, but instead, he looks back at the van like he's in some 1970s disaster movie and he has to leave his beloved behind.

"I'll just stay here and wait for Perlman," he announces.

"What the hell is going on, Jason?" I demand, losing my patience.

"I can't leave the van behind."

And then it hits me.

"*The tree?* Seriously? You're going to stay here in Maine, freeze your ass off, and inconvenience Marie because of a *tree?*"

"It's not just any tree."

"It's a *tree*. You can buy another one easily at some nursery or stand near Mendon."

"None of those are Bessie."

"I'll personally get you whatever tree you want. Have it cut and shipped from Norway, if that's what it takes. You find the best tree you can possibly imagine and I'll–"

"THIS is the best tree, Declan. Bessie. This is it."

"What's so special about this damn tree?"

"It's the tree we planted, the year of the miscarriage."

"The what?"

He moves closer, lowering his voice. "The miscarriage."

"You had a..."

"Yes. It was early, but yes. Happened right before we came here to get our usual tree. And Perlman's grandfather comforted Marie, who was a sobbing mess half the time, though she tried to hide it from the girls. Pops was the one who came up with the idea to plant some trees in honor of the lost little soul."

My admiration for Pops just shot through the stratosphere.

And my sudden commitment to getting old Bessie back to Mendon did, too.

"Come on! It's cold," Andrew shouts, gesturing me toward the helicopter.

Jason looks inside the chopper. The wreath boxes are stacked and cinched tight with a thick vinyl belt. The kids are all in seats, and there's exactly room for the three adults.

"We need a second helicopter," Jason says.

"What?" Andrew shouts.

"Or... no. Just take the tree."

"Take the *tree?* What're you talking about?"

"I'll stay behind. Take the tree in my place."

"Jason, that's crazy talk."

Jordan and Steegan shove over and make room. "You can sit here, Mr. Jacoby! The tree can go there." Steegan points to a spot.

"I am not giving a *Christmas tree* a seat belt spot on my corporate helicopter!" Andrew roars.

"You damn well are," I inform him, climbing out. "I'll give up my seat if I have to."

"What is going on? Is that tree made of gold?"

"It's more precious than that," Jason says.

I give Andrew a look that says, *Go with it. I'll explain later.*

His glare is all I get in return, but he lets out a hefty sigh and moves to help load the damn tree.

"What's the weight on that thing?" the pilot asks me, a pad of paper in hand. He's making quick calculations as we guesstimate the weight of the tree, the wreaths, the kids–all of it.

"We can't make it," I announce, realizing the problem.

"No sh – kidding," Andrew calls out, loud enough for Jeffrey's eyes to gleam with mischief at almost hearing a grown-up curse.

Though, given his mother, I'm sure he hears plenty of profanity at home.

"How about this," I suggest. "Unload the wreaths. Keep the tree and the people. Jason, you said Marie could come up here, right? How about tomorrow you drive up, check in with Perlman about the van, and get the wreaths with your minivan?"

His eyes drift to Bessie.

"We'll bring her," I assure him.

The pilot waves to Andrew, who huddles with him, a sudden thumbs up and a grin from my brother making my spine tingle.

"Problem solved!" Andrew shouts as he reaches for Bessie's trunk, leaning in. "Second helicopter on the way. Pilot called it in when he was landing. Wasn't sure the weight load would work. He can take Jason, the kids, and Jason's crazy tree to Mendon directly. Second helicopter can get us and the wreaths, then deliver the wreaths to Mendon after dropping us off in Boston."

"That's a lot of effort," Jason begins to protest.

"Why is the tree so damn important?" Andrew asks me.

I explain. He goes pale and serious.

"Why didn't he say so in the first place?"

I shrug.

The three of us load Bessie into a seat, Jason clicking her in like a precious child, if by child you mean what looks to be a thirteen-foot tall, six-foot diameter Balsam fir tree. The kids watch, gape-mouthed, as Andrew and I grab the wreath boxes.

"This is insane," Andrew informs me as they begin their lift, the kids waving like crazycakes, Jason giving us a sheepish double thumbs up.

I wave wildly back.

"I know," I shout over the sound of the blades. "It is. But it's the right thing to do. And good thing you can still abuse your Anterdec privileges like this."

"Yeah. Those kids will remember this for the rest of their lives."

"And Jason is eternally in your debt."

"Never hurts to have people owe you favors."

His eyes cut over to me. I groan.

Because I totally owe him now.

And McCormick men never let you forget it.

9

Declan

DIVIDE AND CONQUER ISN'T JUST A BATTLEFIELD strategy.

It's a plan for managing in-laws.

Against my better judgment, and only because I know it pleases Shannon to no end, I've asked Marie to teach me her Yankee Swap ways, and she insisted on taking me shopping. I'm the only person she's showing her secret store to, which is driving Shannon mad.

Except Shannon insists her mother showed her already and can't believe I'm willing to "go to a place like that."

Which has me deeply worried. I've doubled up on hand sanitizer and will update my tetanus booster if needed.

While Marie takes me into the pits of shopping hell and (I hope) back, Jason is spending the day with Shannon and Ellie, helping with a town-wide coat drive for the needy. Grind It Fresh! has been collecting coats, gloves, socks, and hats for the last month, and Dave already sent over our collections, along with a cashier's check. The corporate grants we dispense have already been handed out as part of end-of-quarter books, but

Shannon wanted to add something extra, a personal donation that'll help lighten our taxes, too.

Too bad it's not as easy to get Shannon's family to accept money.

"Declan!" Marie calls out as I ring the doorbell before stepping inside. "Why do you ring the bell? You're family!"

"I know. I do it to warn you."

"Warn me?"

"I don't want a repeat of that whole sofa incident," I say, stomach churning at the memory of finding a shirtless Jason on top of Marie, whose state of undress will remain forever stuck in some part of my brain that went into a fugue state as a form of self-preservation.

I will ring my in-laws' doorbell until the day I'm buried.

"Oh, that?" Laughter tinkles from upstairs like icicles crackling in a sudden snap. "Jason and I were just–"

"Declan!" Saved from what I know was about to be more explicit than the Cardi B song the scouts were obsessed with on our trip to Maine, I find myself giving Jason a manbrace, the half hug, half back-clap my dad is known for. Jason's more of a traditional hugger, so this is odd, but a fine change of pace. "Marie said she was taking you shopping, but I didn't believe her."

"Couldn't believe I'd voluntarily spend an afternoon alone with her?" I joke.

"Exactly."

"Ha ha, Jason! You two are such jokers."

We look at each other. We say nothing.

Marie thumps down the white-carpeted stairs wearing a red Christmas sweater, green leggings with ornaments printed on them, red snow boots up to her calves, and a newly styled mid-length hairdo that screams L.L. Bean catalog, circa before I was born. My mother-in-law is overbearingly loving at best, cloyingly oversharing at worst.

I've never spent an entire day alone with her.

A sudden shiver makes me wonder if there's a grave out there in a parallel life of mine, one Marie's just run across.

"Just let me get my purse and I'll be ready." Her eyes comb over me, from bottom to top. "No suit?"

"Shannon told me to dress casually."

"That means gold cuff links instead of platinum, by your standards." Her wink is salacious.

"Jeans, boots, silk long johns, a cashmere sweater, and a warm coat and gloves are what Shannon said. She warned me we might be outside. What kind of store are we going to that's outside?"

"My secret-weapon store. You'll love it. Huge market out in Spencer." She flashes me a big grin as she heads to the kitchen in search of the leather RV she calls a purse.

Jason gives Marie a sharp look as she walks away, watching carefully. The woman is his beloved wife. Why be so wary?

My hackles rise.

Something's *off*.

Once Marie's gone, he crosses the space between us quickly. He smells like sawdust and shaving cream, a layer of sweat under it.

"Declan."

"Yes?"

"She's lying."

"Who? Marie?"

"Yes."

"Lying about what?"

"That's not her secret thrift shop."

"It's not?"

"Ask Shannon."

"Shannon? How would Shannon know Marie's secret store? Marie told me I'm the only one she's ever–oh, geez."

"Right. Marie's playing you off each other. Carol and Amy, too."

"You're telling me the recycling-center place she told me about isn't her secret weapon?"

"Text Shannon right now and ask her where her mother's secret thrift shop is."

I do as he suggests.

Quickly, my wife replies with: *St. Regis Catholic Church Thrift Boutique in Upton. Why? I thought you said she was taking you there.*

I groan.

"She told Carol it's the Unitarian Universalist youth group's monthly rummage sale. Amy thinks it's the humane society thrift shop in Ashland. See? She's telling you all a different store so she can divide you."

"Why?"

"So she can win."

"But Jason, this is about finding the strangest possible, most fought-over gift for a secondhand gift exchange where the goal is to be the weirdest. Marie already wins that title."

"Hey," he growls. The line with Jason is always there, even if he doesn't draw it starkly. Looks like I crossed it.

"So what is her secret store?"

"Can't tell you."

"But you know."

"Of course, I know. I'm her husband."

"How do you know she isn't lying to you, too?"

"Because she would never..." His voice trails off. Poor guy. Consternation fills his bright blue eyes. "She wouldn't!"

"Bet she did."

One eye squints at me. "Then how do you know Shannon's telling *you* the truth?"

"Why would Shannon lie... *oh*."

A long sigh, then a hand on my shoulder. We're connected by the realization that testosterone is no defense against these estrogen-filled creatures. Instantly, Jason is my best friend.

"Wily women, they are."

"You sound like Yoda."

"They're playing a dangerous game. I don't know who to trust."

"Now you sound like Fox Mulder from *X-Files*."

"Great show!" He peers at me. "Most kids your age don't know about it."

I bristle at the word *kids*.

"Shannon made me watch a few seasons. It's not half bad."

"You watch TV?" He seems shocked.

"You're changing the subject, Jason. You think our wives are engaged in a coordinated disinformation campaign regarding the Yankee Swap so they can outmaneuver me and win."

"I–" His mouth snaps shut. "I guess I do. That just makes it sound so ruthless."

"Because it *is* ruthless!"

"I don't like to think of my little girl and my wife that way."

"Which is why they succeed."

"Ouch!"

"Truth hurts. The faster you accept it and move out of denial, the sooner you'll find a resolution that lets you win."

"Shannon always said *you* were ruthless. More like James than you let on."

"I'm being double crossed by my mother-in-law and my wife over an under-twenty-dollars junk gift. If there's ever a time to be ruthless, this is it."

"No, Declan. If there's ever a time to let it go, this is definitely it," he says back, laughter deepening with each passing second.

He's right.

I can't admit that, though.

Marie returns.

"Ready?" she asks brightly, walking next to me, linking her arm in mine. She bats her eyelashes at me as she says, "I'm off for a day of lunch and shopping with my billionaire boyfriend!"

Jason kisses her cheek and says, "Have fun! Shannon and Ellie are helping with the coat drive, and then we're coming back here and watching the Pats game I taped, so my boyfriend for the day is Bill Belichick."

"Jason," she says, with an aggrieved sigh. "I mean, he's very good at what he does, but if you're going to start dating men, you could set your sights a little–"

"Marie," I say in a low, firm voice, "let's go. And when did lunch become part of the bargain?"

"When you're buying, of course."

It's no secret my mother-in-law loves my money–or the idea of it, anyway. She loves the cachet that comes with being connected to my family, my name, my wealth. And yet... she and Jason, and Carol and Amy, won't let us be overly generous. Shannon's tried to explain it to me over the years, and while I understand it comes down to pride, I think it's more this:

They're not achievers. They don't have the killer instinct that runs through my blood. Was some of it put there by my dad? Sure. But Andrew and I come by it naturally, too.

Terry, less so, but sometimes I think he's the biggest shark of us all.

I escort her out to my new Mercedes SUV, one with a wide backseat that'll easily fit two car seats–soon.

Don't tell her that, though.

"Where are we going, exactly? I know it's in Spencer, but what's the address?"

She gives me the name of the road, and I enter it into the GPS.

"Heated leather seats? Mmmmm," she says as we back out of the driveway.

"Yes, ma'am." Her thrill at what seems like a standard feature is always endearing, even if she's a pain in the ass most of the time.

That's the problem with Marie: She's barely tolerable for long stretches of time and then *bam!* Suddenly, you see a three-dimensional version of her that is touching and connected, and you're left wondering if you're the crazy one.

For the record? I'm not.

"You know, if you and Jason would relent, you could ride around in a car like this, too. I know Shannon's offered. Our money guys set her up with a disbursement. She tries to spend it on you, but you won't let her."

"Shannon calls it her allowance."

I hate that word.

"Listen to you!" Marie says. "Disbursement. So fancy. It's an allowance. Like she's a kid who needs to make a quarter for doing a chore."

"The same term applies to me and Andrew."

"I know. It's just... weird."

"It's money. Shannon has it now. She wants to spend it on you, but you won't let her."

Of all the members of Shannon's extended family, Marie is the one with the worst boundaries and also the biggest ego. Getting her to crack won't be easy, but I have five hours to kill.

Having a goal makes it way more fun.

See? Achiever.

"Jason says if we let her just throw money at us, we'll feel indebted to you."

"So?"

"*So?*"

"Yes. So? You might feel that way, but that doesn't mean I hold it over you."

"Of course you do! You would."

"That's one hell of an assumption."

"It's not an assumption. It's fact."

"No, Marie. A fact is an objective truth. You have no proof, objectively, that our giving you money would mean I would use that against you, or hold it over your head. Do you have any evidence that I've behaved that way in the past?"

"No," she admits reluctantly. "But–but you could."

"Do you use the help you give Carol as some sort of nefarious control mechanism?"

Pure shock covers her face. "Good Lord, of course not!"

"Then why would you think so little of Shannon?"

"I don't!"

"Or is it me? You assume I'm some kind of asshole who will try to dominate you because I gave you money?"

"How did we get on this topic, Declan? I thought we were going to a flea market, not having some kind of financial therapy session."

"Have you ever thought about how guilty Shannon feels?"

I brought a bazooka to a BB gun fight.

Keep in mind that while I have no financial hang-ups whatsoever about giving Shannon's family money, Shannon absolutely does.

And it kills me.

She obsesses over the inequity. Thinks it through from twenty-seven different angles. Invents ways to convince her parents that it's fine to accept what we want to offer, or comes up with complicated plans to make it look like they're doing us a favor by accepting our help.

My job is to listen, occasionally murmur supportive phrases like, "That sounds good," or "They'll definitely find that easier," all the while imagining how easy it would be to just wire some money, pay off all their debts, and stop having to hear my wife loop obsessively about an issue that is, at its heart, so simple.

"Guilty?"

"Mmm."

"Guilty?" she repeats, her voice moving up, as if she's trying to comprehend.

"Yes."

"Why?"

"I'm not the person to ask. I don't understand it, either. My life would be much easier if you'd just accept what we offer and move on with life."

"You offered to give us six figures!"

"Yes."

"People don't just hand out money like that!"

"We do. We can."

She stares at me.

"Marie, your husband rightly won hundreds of thousands of dollars at one of my father's casinos, and used it to pay him back for a perceived debt. You have some serious mental issues with money."

Marie hits my arm, hard. "You take that back!"

"It's the truth."

"I don't have mental issues!"

Ever try to drive while laughing explosively?

"Quit swerving!" she screams as I get myself, and the car, under control.

"You and Jason have some very bizarre ideas about money, accepting it from people, what the word *earn* means, and how family helps each other," I explain to her as it slowly occurs to me that she doesn't know.

She really doesn't know how dysfunctional her view of cash is.

"You can't say that about us. You McCormicks are the ones with the weirdo ideas around money and wealth."

"Our hypercompetitiveness? Sure."

"That's just the beginning, Declan. Your father uses money to control you. Terry walked away from it all and lives a quiet life on more than enough from a trust fund. But you and Andrew tried to prove yourself to James. You had to buy your own chains of businesses to get out from under his thumb and finally start to show yourselves that you could be successful–even when you were already wildly successful before that!"

"How is any of that weird?"

"It's crazy! Who keeps working harder and harder to have more and more, when you already have so much more than most of the world?"

"I don't understand your question."

"No, Declan. You don't accept the *premise* of my question. There's a big difference. You could quit, sell Grind It Fresh!, and live comfortably off your mother's trust fund money and your own assets for the rest of your life, couldn't you?"

My gut twists at the thought.

"No."

"I'm not asking, will you. I'm asking–could you?"

"Live like Terry?"

"Terry lives more comfortably than most people. He certainly makes more than Jason and I do combined."

"How do you know?"

"Shannon told me what you get from your mother's trust. I assume you, Terry, and Andrew each get the same annual amount?"

I nod, surprised that Shannon told her that. Makes sense, though. She shares a lot with her mother.

"Your view of money is skewed."

"No, Marie, *yours* is."

"Anyway, this is all Jason's fault."

"Jason's?"

"His pride. He doesn't want to accept money from James."

"My money is mine. Our money–mine and Shannon's–I mean."

"I know. Shannon keeps offering us some of her allowance. But Jason views it as James's money and worries that if he ever found out, he'd lord it over us."

I open my mouth to object, then snap it shut.

She's not wrong.

"You'd rather live without than deal with my father's warped ideas about money?"

"Listen to you! Warped, bizarre, skewed–you use such negative words when you talk about this."

"Only when I see how the money could help people, but there's an obstacle." The GPS tells me to make a right-hand turn. We're seven minutes from the store. "Like with Tyler."

"Tyler? You already pay for so many of his therapies."

"Sure. And we want to pay for a private school that could help him even more with his issues."

"That wouldn't be fair to Jeffrey."

"We'll cover his tuition, too. Wherever Carol wants. That kid is sharp. He'd thrive at Milton or Deerfield."

"Deerfield Academy? Oh, Declan," she giggles, the laughter fast and full. "You think Carol would ever let Jeffrey go to a boarding school?"

"It's only an hour or so away. He could come home on weekends."

A strange sadness I don't understand twists the muscle above the bridge of her nose. Marie's chin drops and her eyes cut to me, but she doesn't make eye contact. "You think that's okay for a thirteen-year-old boy?"

"*I* was a thirteen-year-old boy who went to boarding school."

A silence as wide as a canyon fills the space between us.

Finally, she asks softly, "And did you like it?"

Instant responses are my forte, so my brain conjures one, the standard positive response right there.

Until it isn't.

"I–"

"And don't say what James programmed you to say. Milton Academy is an absolutely outstanding prep school. It's of the highest calibre, so I'm not asking about the school. I'm asking about *you*. Did you like being away from your mother so much?"

"Like? What does *liking* it have to do with anything?" The GPS says two minutes.

Two minutes that will now feel like two hundred.

"Now you sound just like Jason."

"In what way?"

"Neither of you wants someone controlling how you feel. Jason handles it by rejecting help. You do it by pretending you don't have emotions other people can affect."

"That's ridiculous."

"I KNOW!"

"I meant that your theory is ridiculous."

"So is your behavior."

"I see where your daughter gets it."

"Gets what?"

"Her crazy ideas about how unemotional I am."

"HAH! See?"

"See what?"

"We're right. Shannon and me. We're right about Jason and we're right about you."

"Then prove Jason wrong and accept money from us. Let us make your life easier."

A black chicken runs in front of the car in the parking lot the GPS told me to turn into.

I manage to avoid it, but the front right tire sinks a foot into a pothole that reminds me of a business trip to Ohio in March.

"Parking lot" is a generous term for this rutted expanse of land that was once covered in gravel but is now nothing but dirt and old Dunkin' Donuts cups.

"Where are we?" I ask, looking around. A guy in a day-glo yellow vest waves us toward him, directing me to pull in next to a car he's just guided into a parking spot.

"Park right there," Marie says, pointing. "Then we pay the fee."

"Fee?"

"Don't worry, Moneybags. I've got you covered." She's pulling a twenty-dollar bill out of her wallet when the guy taps on the window.

What kind of store *is* this?

I roll the window down and suddenly, Marie's in my lap, thrusting her arm across my chest. "Hey, Ben!"

"Marie! Whatcha been up to? Haven't seen ya around for a while." He takes the twenty and looks at my car, then me. "You her new boyfriend?" Ben lets out a whistle. "Nice upgrade from Jason."

"BEN!"

Not sure whether the whistle was for me, or the Mercedes.

The guy laughs, a smoker's phlegmy rumble. It lasts a few seconds longer than it should after he stops making voluntary noise. "Just kidding. You the billionaire son-in-law she raves about all the time?"

"Declan McCormick," I say, offering my hand. He shakes it, palms like fish scales.

"Bennett. Ben for short."

"Nice to meet you."

"You, too. Hope you find something good." His eyes take in my car. "Then again, you could just buy everything up and save us all the trouble of selling our crap."

"Ben!" Marie chides again, but smiling.

Another long, loose laugh and Ben turns his attention to the next car.

"What was that?"

"What was what? Ben?"

"You paid him a twenty-dollar fee so we can shop somewhere?"

"Think of it like tipping a valet."

"But he didn't do anything."

"Then think of him like a billionaire sitting at his desk for three seconds and earning twenty dollars."

I ignore that and peer around her.

"That's a store?"

"A flea market."

"It looks like a homeless encampment. I've seen places like this in Seattle and Portland, blue tarps and all. Do you–do you buy strange used items from homeless people and use them for the Yankee Swap?"

"You've been to thrift shops before. This is one."

"It doesn't have a door. Or a roof."

She opens the door and climbs out. "Let me show you the wonders of the flea market, Declan."

"Do I need a vaccination to attend?"

"Oh, stop. Time is of the essence, you know. Christmas is a week away."

"And this is where you find your best Yankee Swap gifts?"

"Yes."

Bright and cheery suddenly, Marie's behavior doesn't square up. We walk across the barren, bumpy lot, a steady stream of cars coming in, lining up for Ben to direct them. There have to be at least a hundred cars already here, at twenty a pop.

"How many people come to this store?"

"It's not a store, it's a flea market! It's like a big, outdoor antiques fair, only people are selling less expensive stuff."

"Okay." The blue tarps tossed over tables don't inspire confidence.

It's clear this place has been built using broken-down buildings; even the tables slant to and fro. A cluster of food trucks behind an old barn is the only sign of modernity around. When I was at Milton, we did a service project in Louisiana after Hurricane Katrina and, minus the water, this place is looking very similar.

"Quit sneering," Marie insists.

"What sneer?"

"That one." She points to my face.

"This is my face without expression."

Heavily made up eyes search mine. "Oh. Huh. Shannon's right."

"About what?"

"You do look like you're simmering all the time."

"Simmering?"

"A little bit angry."

"Shannon said that about me?"

Shifty eyes won't meet mine suddenly. "Maybe."

"You just said she did, Marie."

"Oh, I don't remember who said what! Look! A cable spool turned into a chair, with a cat bed built into it!"

Deflection is an art form, but Marie's version of it is like comparing a toddler's painting to a Jackson Pollock. Just because you give someone a can of paint and tell them to fling it at the canvas doesn't make it a skilled work of art.

In the end, all you have is a giant mess.

"This looks like a shantytown," I inform her. "Something you fly over on your way to Rio."

"You are so stuck up."

"The truth isn't stuck up."

"You're proving my point, Declan." Marie grabs my arm, her touch non-combative. Friendly and connecting. "Look," she says, with eyes that mirror my wife's, not in color but in emotion. "I challenge you to find something meaningful here."

"I'm worried I'll find something *contagious* here."

"Declan. Please. You might be pleasantly surprised."

"By junk?"

"By the meaning that these old items hold. Junk is only junk if it isn't useful or meaningful. Otherwise, it's functional or beautiful. One man's trash is another man's treasure, right?"

"You think I'll find treasure here?"

"Only if you open your mind. And wallet."

"You really think that kind of approach works with me? What is that, some sort of guilt strategy? Guilt and shame?"

"The truth," she says flippantly, using my own words against me.

I laugh in spite of myself and we head toward the junkyard.

Okay. Fine. Flea market.

"Why do they call it a flea market, anyway? Do they fumigate the place before we get started?"

"Good question! Let's ask Sally."

"Sally?"

"SALLY!" Marie screams toward a lump of blankets wearing a Patriots hat, pulling on my arm.

A Cheshire Cat grin spreads under the hat, the woman's forehead sliding up to reveal narrow eyes and a long, thin nose. She takes a long drag off a vape pen and holds it in, then releases cotton-candy-scented breath.

"Hey, Marie. How much *he* cost you? What'd I tell you about bringing a gigolo here with you?"

I turn around to see who she's talking about. No one's behind me.

"This is my son-in-law, Declan," Marie explains. Sally takes another long drag, holds it, then exhales as her eyes check me out from top to bottom.

She winks at me. "Nice cover story. Whatever you gotta do to make a buck, right, buddy?"

"I am not a male escort." That's a sentence I've never had to say before.

"You pay him extra to protest? Nice role play. He's good. You got acting experience?"

Marie turns out to be stronger than I ever realized as she pulls me away from Sally, who she scowls at as we leave.

"She's a little..." Marie twists her finger around her ear.

"What did she mean, *gigolo?*" I put out a palm to halt her before she answers. "And I do not want to know if it involves your and Jason's sex life."

Her lips clamp shut.

That lasts two seconds before she points and says, "Oooo, look! A life-size Tootsie Roll tin!"

And then she proves it's life sized.

By climbing in.

Tempting though it may be to kick the cylinder over and give her a heave-ho for the roll of her life, I watch as Marie chats up the owner of the enormous tin, a guy who shows her his specialty: making foldable tent carts for bicycles out of recycled sofa cushions and military surplus.

My phone rings.

"Dec? Honey? Just tell me where you buried her," Shannon says, her voice reflecting a smile I can conjure instantly in my mind's eye.

"You assume I've killed her already?"

"If you haven't, you have the patience of a saint. I know what Mom's like in a thrift shop."

"We're not in a thrift shop."

Eerie silence greets me. Shannon's voice drops to a lower register. "Where are you?"

"A flea bath."

"A flea bath? Mom took you to a dog groomer? Is something wrong with Chuffy?"

"No. We're at some outdoor market. I've been accused of being Marie's gigolo by a mountain of textiles wearing a Patriots cap."

"Sally?"

"Yes." The fact that she actually knows who I'm talking about shouldn't surprise me, but it does.

"Flea *market,* Dec. Not flea bath."

"Same thing."

"Which one did Mom bring you to?"

"The one that looks like a FEMA disaster area after a hurricane."

"You'll have to be more specific. Sally sells stuff at more than one."

"These things have names? I don't know. The one that reminds me of the tent city on Pearl Street in Portland."

"It's not *that* bad," she scoffs.

"I've seen fewer oddities in a wet market in Beijing."

A Roomba robot vacuum cleaner zips by like an extra in a Star Wars movie, carrying an espresso machine on its back, followed by a tall, frail elderly man screaming, "The press mechanism is stuck! The coffee will taste like dirt!"

I make a mental note for Dave to look into robotics for Grind It Fresh! Promotions.

"We're in Spencer," I tell her.

"That flea market is a little different from most. Lots of makers there."

"Maker's? Like Maker's Mark?" Suddenly, the place is a little more promising.

"No, no. Nothing about alcohol. Makers are people who invent things. They *make*, you know?"

"Why not call them inventors?"

"Because they don't patent their inventions, and..." Her voice trails off. "I don't know why. Good question."

Marie, who is now holding a copper pot with a lobster stamped into the side of it, looks down and shrieks. A wooden box with a net in it catches my eye.

Lobster trap.

"I've been looking for a lobster trap bassinet for so long!" she screeches, giving me a pointed look. "When *someone* has another baby, it'll be the perfect shower gift!"

"I'm sure Andrew and Amanda will appreciate that," I reply.

She halts. "Amanda's pregnant again?"

"Yesssss," I reply with a big grin. This just took a turn toward fun. "Andrew swore me to secrecy, Marie, so please don't tell anyone."

"Oh, of course not! You know me, Declan. You know how I am with secrets."

"I do, yes."

Shifty eyes meet mine. "Um, I'm going to go over to the perfume table."

"Perfume?"

"Jasmine is a perfume thrifter. Buys old perfume bottles and sells them here."

"Used?"

"Of course."

"Isn't there some sanitation code against that?"

"If there is, don't tell anyone! It's how Jasmine covers the difference between her disability check and her expenses." Marie flits off, disappearing around a corner near a big rainbow tie-dyed sheet.

As I pivot away from her, I see just how big–and busy–this place really is. There must be two hundred tables here, each brimming with a different category of wares. Booksellers dominate, followed by people selling assorted glassware and china, then jewelry, all of it reminding me of the cheap costume stuff my mother wore when she was "going casual."

One table is nothing but wooden signs, with kitschy sayings like "If you came to see us, come on in. If you came to see our house, bring a cleaning lady." Now I know where Marie got all the signs at their house.

The sheer variety of junk being sold, but in collections, astounds me. One man sells nothing but tea pots, many of them cracked china, but with price tags that read $10, $25, and Ask for Price. Arrayed in large boxes, they're presented without fanfare, as if the customer is expected to work for his treasure.

A long row of bikes that look like something out of a 1950s sitcom catch my eye. Before I can reach the booth, my phone rings.

It's Shannon.

"AMANDA IS PREGNANT?" she screeches in my ear. I nearly drop the phone, but look at the time instead.

"Four minutes. Marie has more restraint than I thought."

"Mom said you made her swear to keep it a secret."

"And yet here you are, telling me."

"I knew it was a lie." She pauses. "It is a lie, right?"

"Yes."

"Why?"

"Three words: lobster trap bassinet."

Silence greets my pronouncement.

Then, finally, she says: "Quick thinking."

"That's my specialty."

"You realize Mom's going to call Pam next."

"Mmmm."

"Upsetting Pam isn't nice."

"Having Marie let people think I'm her gigolo isn't, either."

"She *what?* Why?"

"The mysteries of your mother's thought process are sewage-filled waters I refuse to wade in, Shannon."

"What do I do? I can't let her think Amanda's really pregnant."

"Why not?"

"Because eventually, Amanda will find out."

"And the problem is?"

"You invented a baby just to get out of a lobster trap bassinet?"

"No jury of my peers would convict me."

"So you want me to let Mom make a fool of herself?"

"She doesn't need any help at all in that department."

"How can you be so cold?"

"If she hadn't told you, she wouldn't be in this predicament."

More silence.

Then she whispers, "She's told Pam by now."

"Likely."

"And Pam will call Amanda."

"Likely as well."

"And Amanda will call me."

"Likely as–"

Beep

"Call coming in from Amanda," Shannon groans. "I can't believe I have to clean up your mess!"

"I love you," I say clearly.

"You're paying for this."

"You never mind my messes in bed."

"At least I get tremendous pleasure from those!"

"Touché."

And she ends the call.

Sunlight shines in a pattern through the rustling leaves of a tree, catching my eye. The breeze makes a changing kaleidoscope of the colored light that dapples the tree trunk and the ground beneath. A quick look nearby shows me a stained-glass vendor, someone selling enormous and highly professional pieces. Wind chimes fill the air with a joyful noise, the designs all stained glass as well, many of them with hand-blown glass beads.

The table stands out, artistically and colorfully.

I'm drawn to it for reasons I don't understand, enthralled by the variety of pieces, body relaxing as I smile.

"Help you find something?" The woman running the table is big boned, tall and thick, but with the kind of body that stays in motion all the time. She's wearing a heavy woven poncho and a thick wool hat knitted like a stained-glass window in a church.

Except Jesus is wearing a Santa hat.

"I'm looking around. Thank you." Kind grey eyes, smart and

evaluative, meet mine. Tight curls congregate above her eyebrows, peeking out from underneath her toque.

"Are you interested in stained glass?" She hands me her card. The address for her studio is in Weston.

"Weston? I grew up there."

"Really? Small world. My father had his studio on the west side, closer to Wayland, for about thirty years. I just took over."

Matilda Ehrenright.

"Matilda?"

"Tillie."

"Nice to meet you. I'm Declan." No idea why I'm being so friendly. There's something about her. About the glass.

Or maybe this flea market is on a Superfund site and I'm being overcome by odorless toxic fumes.

"My mother used to do this." I point to a mosaic and smile. "All of this reminds me of her."

"It's addictive. Once you start, you can't stop."

"You're a stained-glass artist like your father?"

She shakes her head sadly. "No. I never had the eye for it."

"Then why are you here?"

"Selling it off."

"All this?" There have to be a hundred pieces, from ornaments the size of a drink coaster to full-size windows and doors.

"I drag it around in my truck. Dad's studio had a following."

"I would think your clientele would be a bit more... upscale."

That gets me a raucous laugh. "You would think, wouldn't you? Dad's studio was what he called a working studio. People went for classes, workshops, and a good cup of tea."

"Tea?"

Nostalgia, and a little grief, softens her eyes. "Dad was an artist, but I think his greatest work was in making people feel like they were at home. He built communities as much as he created glass. Some of the people who came to his workshops were good friends. Small groups formed. The women went on vacations together. He was a one-man community center." Her head dips down as she shakes it slowly. "Dad credited himself with six marriages–students who met in his classes."

"Huh. I wonder if my mother was one of his students."

"If you lived in Weston and she did stained glass, there's a really good chance." Tillie pauses. "Was?"

"She passed away."

"I'm so sorry. Recently?"

"No. About fifteen years ago."

"Which means she's really gone."

"Excuse me?"

"I–this sounds rude, but I've been saying the wrong thing most of my life, and this is probably not much different, so here goes: Was it more raw in the beginning? It feels like Dad isn't really gone." Her eyes start to glisten. She widens them, as if trying to dry them out.

Oh, no.

"Um..."

"Sorry. Sorry! You were just a kid, right? You can't be more than thirty."

I chuckle, surprised by how easy it is to talk to her. "I'm older than that, but thank you. She died my senior year of high school."

"Wow. Dad died the day I defended my dissertation."

"Oof."

"Yeah. He was so proud of me. English Lit. What'm I going to do with a PhD in English Lit, other than managing a restaurant or teaching at a prep school?" Palms up, she spreads her hands across the table. "Hence my summer of flea markets and craft fairs. Dad's work is covering my student loans."

Instantly, I decide to buy something from her.

Anything.

"What's the craziest piece you have?"

"What?"

"I'm here with my mother-in-law. She's teaching me the ways of the flea market. We're shopping for goofy gifts for the family Yankee Swap."

"Oh, how fun!"

"My goal is to give the most insane gift. Can you help me?" I wink at her. "Guaranteed sale."

Eyes flashing with merriment and not tears this time, Tillie looks around, then crouches. "How about dogs playing poker?"

"You have that?"

"I have the strangest piece you can imagine." Her voice is muted as she bends under a table, pulling on plastic bins. "It's about two feet by three feet, and it seems to be a group project.

Four dogs playing poker, but a different student did each dog, with the poker table in the middle. Dad must have assembled the pieces and smoothed out the design so it looks like a single, full picture. Composition is great. They're signed, and there's a card that says Weston Conservation Society on the back."

"Dogs playing poker? Isn't that a velvet painting joke?"

"Some group of students turned it into a stained-glass joke."

"Wait. Did you say Weston Conservation Society?"

"Yeah. Dad told me before he died that over the years, when people bought student projects like this at auctions, they often quietly gave them back to him. I'm guessing spouses didn't like the art. He stored them in his back room. Never wanted his students to feel bad."

"And now you're selling those projects?"

Defensiveness creeps into the way she holds her shoulders. "Gotta pay the bills."

"Not judging. In fact, that dogs-playing-poker project might be just the ticket for my Yankee Swap domination."

"Domination?"

"I'm in it to win it."

"Isn't that a bit much for a simple Yankee Swap?"

"What do you mean?"

"Yankee Swaps are about fun. Not who wins."

"Everything in life is a competition."

"You don't hear that very often at a flea market."

"People like me don't tend to go to flea markets."

Tilting her head slightly, she narrows her eyes. "Am I supposed to know you? Are you famous?"

"No." Not yet.

"What do you do for a living, Declan? You sell cars?"

"Coffee."

She brightens. "Ah! My favorite drug. What kind?"

"Have you heard of a coffee chain called Grind It Fresh!?"

"Heard of it? I singlehandedly keep them in business. I'm broke, but I can't resist those roasted cacao chai lattes. And you have the full-fat coconut milk without preservatives, blended with the cashew milk. Whoever came up with that drink is a genius!"

"That would be Dave," I mutter.

"You must be a higher-up there if you know the name of the person who invented the drink."

"I like working there," I say, the vague comment working as she finds the artwork and pulls it out.

I'm stunned.

"It's... breathtaking."

"Oh, my. Someone taught you tact, didn't they?" she says with a loud laugh.

Four dogs, all wearing poker visors, surround a center poker table, green felt brilliantly transposed into glowing stained glass. The upper left corner shows a Chihuahua. Upper right, a black Lab. Lower right, a bichon frise, like Marie's dog, Chuffy.

And the lower left is a black Scottie dog.

"That one." I point. "He looks so much like one of our dogs growing up." The corner of the glass has some cracks in it, as if it's been dropped, but the actual art is unblemished.

Before Tillie can answer, a shrill female voice behind me screams, "CHUFFY!"

Marie has found me.

"Oh, my goodness, Declan! That's quite the piece." She looks at Tillie. "I'll take it!"

Impulse makes me grab the corner of the frame. "It's mine. Too late."

Tillie may have just finished her PhD in a frou-frou subject, but she's a businesswoman at heart. Prying it out of my hands, she holds it up to us both. "Looks like we have a bidding war."

I snort. "Whatever she offers, I'll double it."

Tillie cozies up to Marie and whispers, "Offer five grand."

Marie opens her mouth. I give her a look.

She shuts her mouth.

If only it were always this easy.

"That lower corner looks just like my Chuffy-Wuffy!"

"I was buying this for the Yankee Swap."

"Oh!" Marie brightens. "Then you go right ahead and buy it. I'll fight everyone to the death for it on Christmas."

"You people are brutal," Tillie murmurs. "Who turns a Yankee Swap into a blood sport?"

"We do," Marie and I say in unison. She tries to high five me.

I ignore her.

"How much?"

"You go first," Tillie counters.

"I don't know the value range, so you throw out a number and we'll go from there."

"May I?" Marie asks, reaching for the piece. Tillie hands it off to her and crosses her arms over her chest, clearly unsure what to do, but quite aware that there's more to be made on this than she expected.

Finally, she says, "Five hundred."

Marie gasps. "We have a twenty-dollar limit!"

"You do. I don't," I inform her.

"That's cheating!"

My eye catches the lower left corner again. The Scottie dog has one floppy ear and a little patch of white under the eye, just like Kilty, our old family dog.

"Four hundred," I toss out, fine with five and intending to buy more from Tillie. Shannon would call it a soft spot.

I call it good manners.

"Declan." Something in Marie's voice makes my spine tingle, hands clenching into fists, unreality crawling over my skin.

"Yes?"

She's holding a small piece of paper that was tucked into the back, a bifold the size of a thank-you note. She whispers a word I never expected to hear in a flea market, of all places.

My mother's name.

"Elena," Marie says, reading the card. "'Project made at the Ehrenright Studio and donated to the Weston Conservation Society auction. May 23, 1999.' And it's signed by five people. Elena Montgomery McCormick is one of them." Marie points as she offers me the card.

"Who is she?" Tillie asks, defensiveness gone, the deep curiosity of someone who finds the world fascinating now fully engaged.

"My mother." The words come out hard, visceral, stuck in my throat.

Tears fill Marie's eyes as she solemnly grabs my arm, head tipping down. "Oh, Declan. You found a piece of her you didn't know was out there."

A long sigh comes out of Tillie, the kind of sound that carries scores of emotions in a ratio no one can pinpoint. She reaches for a long strip of bubble wrap. "It's yours. Free."

"Of course not! I'll pay." I reach into my back pocket for my wallet and pull out my cash.

Her eyes widen. "That's quite a bankroll."

"It should be," Marie chirps. "He's a billionaire, after all."

Tillie's laugh is contagious. Hopefully, it's the only thing that is, here at the flea market.

"Billionaire. Right."

"Declan McCormick," Marie says proudly. "Of Anterdec. And now he owns–"

I cover her mouth with my hand. "This beautiful stained-glass artwork." Slowly, I remove my hand from Marie's mouth and give her a look that says *shut up*.

If I were a bookie, I wouldn't take bets on this working, but I have to try.

"Here."

Tillie looks at the five hundred-dollar bills in my hand with wonder.

"You–seriously? You're a McCormick? *The* McCormicks?"

"Yes."

"Then you're the one who owns Grind It Fresh!"

"See?" Marie gives me an exasperated look. "You didn't have to shush me!"

"I–"

"I *hate* when you shush me," Marie adds, looking so much like Tyler, I start to laugh.

Tillie offers one of the hundreds back. "Make you a deal. You get the art for four hundred, I get half off all my drinks at Grind It Fresh! for a month."

I grab my phone and text Dave.

Tillie frowns. "What're you doing?"

"Matilda Ehrenright, yes?"

"Sure."

"What's your phone number? The one you downloaded the app to?"

She pulls her phone out and taps. "You're serious?"

"I just need your number."

She recites it. I type it into the text to Dave.

Bzzz

"Done. Half off all drinks for life."

"Life?"

With my index finger, I stroke the outlines of Kilty. The little dog died in 1999. Andrew and Kilty were inseparable when we were little. That dog slept in his bed with him. Mom loved him so much, too. I wonder if Mom made this in tribute?

"Yes. For life. You've given me something invaluable."

"So have you! Thank you so much, Declan!"

"Thank *you*."

A grandiose, overly loud throat clearing makes us turn and look at my mother-in-law, whose eyebrows are so high, they might as well be a halo.

Or horns.

"If you're handing out gratitude, where's mine?"

"Excuse me?"

She nudges me. "I told you to keep your mind open, and that you might find something meaningful here."

I reach down and kiss her cheek. "You were right."

"You'll have to say that again in front of Jason."

"I will."

"*And* Shannon."

"Fine," I grind out as Tillie giggles and begins wrapping the piece.

"And Amy, and Carol, and–"

"Marie?"

"–Agnes and–"

It's going to be a long day.

10

D*eclan*

Dinner tomorrow. The Fort. My table. Seven p.m. Just you, no Shannon, Dad texts.

You're lucky I'm free, I text back. *Make sure there's a highchair for Ellie.*

No Ellie.

You didn't say that up front.

Don't be pedantic, Declan. It's never suited you.

That's because you hogged allllll the pedantic in the world, Dad, I want to type back, but I hold off.

What's this about? I ask instead.

Doubt creeps in as I re-read his texts. Dad isn't this good a typist. An assistant is entering these for him.

An assistant he's likely entering, too. Dad's taste for young women is legendary, but he's even better known for his willful helplessness.

That's right. Willful helplessness.

Shannon gave me the term for it, a phrase that fits my father to a T. Why do something you don't want to do when you can pretend to be unable and get others to do it for you?

James McCormick, professionally helpless when it comes to tasks he just doesn't want to bother doing.

The boss in the office who can never figure out how to use the copier? Willful helplessness.

The guy who emails you to send a group email to others? Willful helplessness.

The manager who insists he can't get the same result when he calls for an order of some shipment, but you can do it so much better?

Same.

It's a skill. And you know what?

It's a skill I've acquired.

Shannon rages against willful helplessness, but here's what she doesn't understand: It's a form of focus. Intentional focus. In a world where we have too many petty demands placed on us to perform rituals and tasks that don't advance achievement, how do you avoid being swallowed by all that?

You play dumb.

And when playing dumb doesn't work, you condescend and order.

Is it fair? No.

Is it kind? Absolutely not.

Does it accomplish the goal?

Yes.

And I learned from the best: James McCormick.

Be there, his next text reads, and I tap out of the screen. Within seconds, a new text appears, the calendar entry confirmation coming through.

See? His assistant sent that. She's the one who pivoted and created the appointment in the system that auto-notes it in my schedule.

Dad couldn't use integrated text apps if his life depended on it.

I frown at my screen.

What is this meeting about, anyhow?

Bzzz

Speaking of calendar entries, mine is reminding me it's ten minutes before a training session at Old Jorg's gym.

I mean, *my brother's* gym. He bought the regional chain from Old Jorg last year, but I still haven't made the mental shift.

Outside my office, ambulance sirens wail, although the noise is muted. It's a testament to the soundproofing of the building, but nothing completely drowns out emergency services in a downtown setting.

Tap tap tap

Before I can call out an invitation to enter, my gorgeous wife's head pops in.

"Dec?"

"Mmm?" I start removing my suit jacket, loosening the knot in my tie. Her eyes widen with appreciation and I can't help but smile at her reaction.

"What's up?"

Considering the way she's looking at me, *plenty* is up.

"I'm headed to the gym to work out. Vince, Gerald, and Andrew. Standard punishment for an hour. You need something from me?" While I talk, I unbutton my shirt, pulling it out from the waistband. Shannon rests her hip against a credenza by the wall, the pen in her hand going to her mouth as her tongue pokes out to lick it.

"I do need something from you," she says in a breathy voice.

My sex calculator does the math, a quick operation that leads to a simple product: It's been three days since we made love, and it was a hurried affair, interrupted by a toddler cutting a tooth.

And Shannon's ovulating soon.

Bzzz

I look down at my phone screen. It's a text from Dave.

Shannon's peak conception dates start tomorrow.

How the hell does he *do* that?

I take off my shirt, hanging it neatly on the back of my chair, the tie earning a place on my desk. Kicking off my shoes, I start to unbuckle my belt.

Is that a moan I hear from my wife?

"I assume you came here for some reason other than ogling me?"

"Isn't that a good enough reason?"

I realize the second I touch my belt that something else is about to be unleashed, too. Something bigger.

And growing by the minute.

Shannon clicks the door lock. She crosses the room and sets a folder on the chair across from me. Then she angles her body between me and my computer, gently pushing it back so she can sit on the edge of the desk, pulling my ass so I'm between her legs.

"How about this reason?" she asks, splayed palms on my chest, eyes centered on me as she leans in to plant a tiny bite on my nipple.

"That is a fantastic reason," I answer, throat choked with surprise, full-roar desire–and conflict. The guys are waiting for me and I know that if I have any hope of meeting them on time, this has to be fast.

Lightning fast.

But that's why they call it a quickie, right?

My belt's already unbuckled, so as Shannon unzips me, my hands cupping her breasts under the thin sweater she's wearing, her job is easier than mine. I'm bareass and standing at attention as she spreads her legs, my hand moving under her skirt to her soft inner thigh, fingers sinking into the warm, wet, welcoming divine as she surprises me yet again.

No panties.

"You planned this?" I rasp as she pulls her skirt the rest of the way up and guides me in. Christmas jazz is playing through the ceiling speakers, and twinkling lights from the live tree by the credenza give my office a warm glow that enhances the pleasure of taking my lovely wife for a nooner on my desk.

She arches, walls clenching to pull me in deeper as she kisses me, the rolling allure of her tongue making my hands move over her fine hips, fingers gripping her to me, pulling in as my strokes gain momentum, her gasp urging me on. She sits up and I wrap my arms around her, her own rhythm gaining speed until she freezes, shivering with the silent tightness that makes me come instantly, her teeth digging into my shoulder, our slick heat making the conquest of my climax a worthy venture that only took–

I look at the wall clock–

Less than two minutes.

If a guy's going to have a personal best for an achievement, this one is specious. "Faster than a speeding bullet" may be Superman's tagline, but this is one time when being Clark Kent is my preference.

"God, I needed that," Shannon says as she kisses my collarbone, hands sliding down slowly, ending at my navel. Staring up into my eyes, she gives me a fuzzy, unfocused look that sharpens as we lock gazes.

"That was pleasantly unexpected."

"You're the one who started the striptease," she smiles.

"That never works at home."

"Because you do it when Ellie's in the bath!"

"Picky, picky."

She slides off the desk and straightens her skirt, patting her ass and turning herself in circles like a dog chasing its tail.

"What are you doing?" I ask as I shrug into my black workout shirt.

"Making sure we didn't leave any stains on me."

"It would be a badge of honor."

"Gross, Dec!"

"Besides, you can just call Evie to send over a new outfit."

"From Vegas? Haven't thought of her in a while."

"She's opened a boutique here in Boston."

"Really? How would you know?"

"She's sharp. Contacted Andrew and me a while ago. Asked for some co-branding with Anterdec with bathrobes, and wanted to discuss long-term Grind It Fresh! initiatives in fashion."

"Fashion? The closest we get to fashion is the t-shirts in the store."

Bzzz

My phone. It's Andrew.

You're late, is all the text says.

I shove myself into workout shorts, then peel off my socks and throw them on the floor while slipping into gym socks and shoes. Shannon watches the ricochet of black dress sock balls with dismay on her face.

"Gotta run. Love you," I say, giving her a kiss on the cheek. "Thank you."

"You reek of sex! You're going to get all hot and sweaty and the guys will notice."

"Good. Helps me to retain my position as head of the pack."

Raucous, unleashed laughter fills my office as I leave.

It's a little too boisterous.

Old Jorg's gym (I'll never stop calling it that) is close enough that I yank the glass door open at 4:09, earning a glare from Vince and a disappointed head shake from Andrew.

"Hey, Declan," comes from Gerald, who's curling eighties like he's putting a lollipop to his mouth.

Vince's eyes narrow as I grab the water bottle from my bag and fill up at the cooler.

"You look... hollow."

"Huh?"

"Hollow. Empty."

The smirk takes over my face. Hey, can I help it if I feel good? After what Shannon just did, wouldn't you?

All three guys groan in unison.

"You just had sex," Vince says, the curl of his lip showing his disgust.

"Yeah? So? What's wrong with that."

He sniffs. "*Just*."

I shrug. "Is it my fault I'm so magnetically virile, my wife can't help herself?"

Gerald drops the weights, my brother giving him a look that says *screw this guy*. We all have little ones at home–Andrew has two–but there's a world of difference between our two-and-a-half-year-old and their kids' ages.

Shannon and I have more than a year's jump on them, and we've gotten past the bone-weary, no-sleep phase.

Although we're about to re-enter it, if my sperm have any say in the matter.

"I do not want to talk about sex," Andrew grinds out.

"Can't talk about what you don't have?"

Vince's gaze goes to the enormous monster truck tire he makes us play tug-of-war with when he doesn't approve of our conversation. I'm depleted enough that I'd lose. I need rage to win against Andrew, and right now, he's far and away ahead of me in the fury department.

Rightly so.

But why not push some buttons?

"How long's it been?" I ask. I just get an eye roll, so I shove my bag under a bench and take a good look around the gym. Since Andrew acquired the chain last year, he's made very few changes. The goals now are data collection, maintaining existing clientele, and using marketing pushes to grow to capacity before expanding the brand.

Plus, he has twin sixteen-month-olds at home, is withdrawing from Anterdec, and Dad refuses to acknowledge he exists.

Actual pity forms in a dark chamber of my heart. No sex on top of all that?

Poor guy.

"You need the gloves if you're going to use cryo," Vince says to Andrew as he turns away and walks over to a small cabinet.

"Cry-o? Is that what Andrew does after I beat him?"

"It's what you did after Dad picked me to be CEO of Anterdec," Andrew shoots back.

"Something you just tossed in the trash can," I remind him. "How's the disentangling going?"

He ignores that. Seven months ago, Andrew quit his job as CEO of Anterdec. A regular job requires two week's notice, a month or more for higher-ups, but CEO?

You live, breathe, eat, and nearly sleep with your job.

It can take a year, more like two, to leave.

Which also means it's been half a year of silent treatment from our father.

"Let's talk about cryo," Vince persists, returning with gloves.

"What is it?"

"Cryotherapy," Andrew says in a voice that carries the first spark of energy I've heard since I walked in the door.

"You want to freeze me into suspended animation, but I have to take a shower first?"

"If freezing you would shut you up, I'd have done it decades ago."

"Cryotherapy," Vince says loudly, trying to drown us out and succeeding, "is a non-invasive workout enhancer that puts your body in temperatures as low as negative 220 Fahrenheit."

"There's cold shrinkage, and then there's *cryo* shrinkage," Gerald jokes, earning him a silencing look from Vince.

"What's the benefit?" I ask.

"Other than shrinking your balls to subatomic levels?" Andrew asks.

"Too late for you two," Vince deadpans.

"Enough with the insults," I challenge him. "If I wanted to take shit from a guy, I'd spend more time with my dad."

For some reason, I don't mention tonight's dinner with him to Andrew.

"True enough," Andrew concurs.

"Mitochondria," Vince announces, as if that answers everything.

"What?"

"Mitochondria. Using cryotherapy helps with energy use, post-workout recovery, and proper functioning of the mitochondria. And best of all: no chemicals. No 'roids, no supplements, no pressure on the detox system. No liver or kidney involvement. You just strip down and freeze yourself to health."

"This is a machine?"

Andrew nods. "We've got them in four gyms now as a pilot program. Old Jorg approved."

"Why would you need his approval? He doesn't own the gyms anymore."

"Brought him on as a consultant."

"He's ancient! What's he an expert in? Using the Yellow Pages to find a phone number? How to stretch the cord on a wall phone for privacy?"

"You'd be surprised. He really gets gym rats. There's an art to understanding them."

"Does that scale up?"

"I think it will. We've had him talk to some digital marketing experts who are converting his deep subject-matter expertise into the social media space, and so far, so good."

"Old Jorg's one-to-one community approach converted to click-through rates and conversion? There's something unseemly about that."

"Shannon has really gotten to you, hasn't she?"

"Huh?"

"You're going soft, bro."

"What does that mean?"

"You care about the personal touch being lost. That's so Shannon."

"Get in that damn Jorg-approved machine and let's turn you into Han Solo."

Laughing, Andrew walks over to the cylinder, which looks like a very small grain silo with dry ice in it, the fog rolling up as if it's formed by witch's brew. Vince pushes some buttons on a panel, then hands Andrew thin white gloves and another pair of thicker ski gloves. When I look down, I see Andrew's wearing thick socks.

"Thermal stress is critical. We want that brown fat to work for you." Vince's words make no sense, but Andrew climbs in the machine anyhow.

My brother, the guinea pig. He's always been fixated on fitness in a way I wasn't. Sports? Absolutely. Working out to stay strong and in shape? Sure. There's an evolutionary advantage to that.

And a business advantage. Walking into a high-stakes meeting with your core tight, arms pumped, and the power surge that comes from knowing you're going to walk out the winner is a state you can only achieve by being in peak condition.

But Andrew?

He's a bit extra.

More than a bit, actually.

Maybe it's the whole almost-Olympic swimmer thing. Dad lavished attention on Andrew when he got close to making it. Maybe the high-intensity coaching got into his psyche so young, he still craves it. Moving the needle a fraction of a millimeter to gain a tiny, almost undetectable advantage at the Olympic level means going places mere mortals won't go.

I also think it's a giant waste of time.

But my now-bodiless brother doesn't.

"My body hair is snapping off and forming little piles around my feet," Andrew announces. I can't tell if he's joking.

"You said that last time, and you don't look like you bathed in Nair. Just keep moving," Vince snaps at him.

"Moving?"

"He has to walk lightly. Maximizes the benefits."

"Do you optimize everything?"

"Why wouldn't I?"

Five years ago, I wouldn't have even asked Vince that question. His frame of mind is one I know all too well, because I've been there.

Was there.

For most of my adult life.

Have I gone soft? Is the killer instinct leaking out of me, one Daddy hug at a time?

"Love the rush," Andrew says. His head moves up and down slightly as he slowly walks in place. Fog billows up, his eyes widening, a small smile on his face.

"Rush?" I ask, curious now.

"Cryo repairs the tears that intense exercise, especially lifting, causes. It reduces inflammation. Gives you a post-workout rush."

"Nice."

"And no drugs. No supplements. Just cold." Vince is a purist. I can appreciate that.

"What's the market like for this?" I ask, leaning against the wall.

"Small now. Growing, though. People are opening their eyes to contamination."

"Contamination?"

"Chemicals. Pollution. Unnecessary things we put in our bodies that don't need to go there. The future is clean, Declan. Remember? Clean. When you're developing products and culture at Grind It Fresh!, use that as your guide. Dave understands, and we're still working on the deal for your two companies. No one wants flavored crap anymore. They want the real thing, even if it costs more, because people view their bodies as investments now."

"Not all people."

"No. Not all. But the ones you want as customers do, and–"

BEEP!

The cryo door opens and Andrew steps out, hands curling into fists as he heads over to a stationary bike.

"Slow warmth," Vince cautions as my brother, always the overachiever, begins pedaling furiously. At Vince's words, he slows down.

Barely.

For the next twenty minutes, I do my routine, overlapping for ten of those with Gerald. It's arms day, so by the time I'm done, the cryo chamber looks tempting.

Until I check the time.

"I have to go," I say, at the exact moment Andrew says the same words.

He frowns. I frown.

"Seven o'clock meeting," we say, in unison again.

"I thought Andrew's *kids* were the identical twins. Not that you guys are twins," Vince cracks.

"We're busy guys," Andrew mutters.

Andrew runs out the door with barely another word, while I use the showers to get ready. Andrew's first major renovation was to seriously upgrade the locker rooms. Heated tile floors, plenty of hot water, grout that doesn't look like a science experiment, and free towel service make using the gym on your lunch hour, or as a way station between business appointments, far more appealing.

Even Old Jorg approved.

As I button up the business shirt I have in my gym bag, the wrinkles catch my eye. Dad will notice. Not that I care, but the thought floats through my mind, an irritant that tells me some inner sliver of my younger self is paying attention.

There was a time when I did care.

And it stays with me.

I take a quick look in the mirror. I have to turn all the inner critics off, the ones planted there years ago by Dad's glances, brow downturns, curls of the corner of a mouth, an eyelid twitch. We pick up on emotional signals other people put out, radar constantly on, feeling our way through life by sensing the unspoken reactions of others.

Dad has no problem being a straight shooter. Words that cut deep are plentiful there.

Why the dinner? Alone?

Ambushes happen with my father. Is this one of them? Or am I worrying myself for no good reason? When Shannon and I first met, her emotional intelligence struck me, but it was buried under too many years of having her enthusiasm for life and connection thwarted by a bad relationship with a guy who didn't see what a treasure she was. Add in a family that overshares and overreaches, and Shannon was a worry-wart with a heart of gold and really good instincts about people.

In marriages, they say, you take on each other's traits over time. Shannon got a bit of my backbone and a heaping dose of my boundaries to help her as she grows.

She gave me a child. No competition there. She wins.

But I think I got the short end of the stick in the emotional part, because over time, some of her worry has crept in.

Open at the throat, my shirt looks fine under the jacket as I straighten up, running the comb through my hair one more time. I briefly consider the rolled-up tie in my bag. Dad will critique my wrinkled cotton, and definitely the twelve hours of beard growth I'll display when I arrive.

So what?

If he's going to find one thing to criticize, I might as well go for breaking all his rules.

No tie, then.

Zipping up the bag, I stuff it in the locker I rent there and start on my walk to The Fort, feeling good about the workout. I don't need the six-block walk for exercise.

I do need it to clear my head.

For the last half a year, Dad's gone full silent treatment on Andrew, pretending he simply doesn't exist. The twins' first birthday party was a mess, with Dad attending, Pam cajoling, Amanda in tears, and tension so thick you couldn't cut it with a knife–you needed a chainsaw.

Being summoned by James McCormick is never good.

Being summoned while he's in month seven of not speaking to his closest child feels post-apocalyptic.

What kind of dressing down am I about to get?

Worse–will he make some crackpot demand that I ignore Andrew, too?

The Fort holds a nostalgic place in my heart. The restaurant is one of the flagships in the Anterdec portfolio, but it's also where Shannon showed me what a dumbass I was being.

And her best friend got my brothers and father to help out with the effort.

Breaking up with Shannon while we were dating simply because she has a bee allergy, much like the allergy that killed my mother, was reckless and stupid. I used to think that being closed off was a form of strength.

Shannon's shown me it's exactly the opposite. Vulnerability is a superpower.

And yet, I can't display it with my father.

"Mr. McCormick?" The maitre d' smiles at me as I walk in through the thick wooden doors and stride up to the desk. I can't remember his name.

"I am. Is the other Mr. McCormick here?"

"They both are, indeed."

Both?

I nearly say the word aloud, but pull back sharply. Both? Dad invited Andrew, too? Is this Andrew's seven o'clock meeting?

As I follow the maitre d' through the restaurant, the past washes over me. There's the hallway where I kissed Shannon at a business event, the feel of her as I pushed her against the wall delicious and visceral. Then there's that time I showed Dad the engagement ring before I proposed to Shannon.

Those are the feelings I want to cultivate.

The positive ones.

And they're always about her, aren't they?

As it should be.

Dad doesn't look up as we approach, and the guy who is sitting with him is not Andrew. Longish hair with a slight wave, and thick as all get out–with a sprinkle of silver in there–tells me exactly who's sitting with Dad.

"Terry?"

He turns and gives me a wide-eyed, *Can you believe this?* look as he stands and pulls me in for a brotherly hug. Before we separate, he whispers, "Ambush."

Huh. So I'm not the only one who thinks that way.

"Dad," I say politely as he continues to ignore us, fixated on his phone. I sit, give my drink order (Balvenie, neat), then turn to my brother.

"You look very strange in a suit."

"That's because I feel very strange in a suit."

"Why wear it?"

"Dad asked me to."

"Since when do you listen to him?"

That finally gets Dad's attention, just as my drink is smoothly placed in front of me. Perfect timing.

"You two think you're so smart," Dad grouses as he takes his own glass and hoists it into the air in a toast. Terry's drinking beer, I've got my scotch, and we go along with whatever this game is, even if we don't know the rules.

Because we know which team we're on.

And it's not Dad's.

"To Anterdec," Dad says loudly before downing his whisky.

Terry and I don't repeat the toast, but we most certainly finish our drinks.

Fast.

A charcuterie board in front of Terry gives me something to do with my hands as Dad watches us, eyes pinging to and fro.

"I've ordered the surf and turf for us all. You know Dominic makes the best filet." Dominic is the master chef, a guy who has been running the kitchen forever, but I also know that the second-in-charge, Samil, has introduced a variety of dishes that help expand the restaurant's clientele beyond guys who think the Rat Pack was the height of entertainment sophistication.

"I don't eat red meat, Dad," Terry says amiably. "But I'll enjoy the lobster."

"What do you have against cows?"

"Nothing. I like them so much, I don't want to kill them."

An eye roll, a scowl, and a snort all emerge from Dad in response. It's the emotional version of the dark triad.

"How's my granddaughter?" Dad asks me as I sample the olives.

"She's great. You'll see her at Christmas. She loves her twin cousins."

At the mention of his grandsons, Dad softens. "I saw them last week, at Pam's. We took them for a walk. They have strong little legs and long torsos like your brother."

Terry tenses. I've heard it all before. He hasn't. And he knows Dad.

Knows exactly what this means.

"Andrew spends a lot of time with them in the pool," I venture, pushing the tension up a notch on purpose. Unlike Dad, I'm not playing this ridiculous game of pretending my brother doesn't exist.

A grunt is all we get. Terry looks at me as if to ask, *He's still giving Andrew the silent treatment?*

I nod as I eat a roasted fig wrapped in bacon.

"It's loud and crazy and fun when we get the little kids

together. Terry, you need to come over again. We haven't seen you since Labor Day."

He smiles. "Uncater needs to see them all more."

"Unc-a-tair?" Dad repeats.

"Ellie's nickname for me," Terry explains, loosening his tie, earning a raised eyebrow from Dad. The server delivers a bread-basket and a fresh whisky for Dad.

"Uncadoo is what she calls Andrew," I say, goading the old man into saying something about our brother. You know–his son? The one he handed his entire company to five years ago?

"I enjoy being called Grandpa by all of the children." His eyes go unfocused, from nostalgia or whisky. With Dad, it's hard to tell the difference, but even Terry pays him a little more attention. Table scraps of emotion are all we get from our father, and while we're both wise enough to know this, we're still hard-wired to want whatever we can get.

"How does it feel?" Terry asks before grabbing some bread and dipping it in olive oil with red pepper flakes.

"Grandfatherhood? It feels exactly as I'd imagined. I'm old. They're toddlers who scream and whine and smell funny when their diapers are full. But I'm spry and can pick them up and turn into a lovable old goof without judgment, so I am fulfilling my end of the bargain."

Lovable old goof.

When has James McCormick ever been a lovable old goof? Or without judgment?

"I'm glad you have that, Dad," Terry replies, words tender but distant. He sounds like a crisis therapist offering a band-aid of support to someone they'll never see again.

"I am too, no thanks to you."

"Excuse me?"

"You have not produced an heir."

"Ah, geez," Terry says, stripping off the tie and shoving it in his front pocket, the gesture clear: He's done with pretense.

I'm surprised he ever allowed himself to engage in any to begin with.

Salads are served, small requisite dishes that are clearly just placeholders, a mere suggestion of a dinner course for the sake of protocol. Five bites and I'm done, the scotch doing nothing for my tension.

Pretty sure I could bathe in it and still feel like a walking slab of granite.

As Terry looks around, he's clearly processing what he's taking in, the restaurant's old-world feel still intact. Not much has changed since the days when he worked for Anterdec, back when he was the rightful heir.

"I can't believe it still looks the same here," he finally says, proving I'm a mind reader.

"That's how it should be. Keep the atmosphere. The menu is updated, though. And behind the scenes, we have state-of-the-art computer systems. We're high tech where it counts." Dad cocks his head, studying Terry a bit. "Good to see you care."

"I don't. Just observing."

"You care more than you'll admit."

"Care about what?"

"The company."

"Where's this coming from? I haven't worked for Anterdec in... well..."

Since Mom died.

No one will say it, but we're all thinking it.

"We should remedy that."

Dad's words make both of us sit up taller, Terry's body suddenly bigger, thicker, stronger than I've seen in years. My older brother used to be my idol. I worshipped him. Wanted to be him. Knew he was destined for the CEO position at the family company, and appreciated it.

Because I was the spare. Terry was the heir.

Then I screwed up, in Dad's eyes, and listened to our mother. After that, I could do no right.

And Andrew was the Golden Child.

So what's this all about now?

"Can't remedy something that doesn't need to be healed," Terry says slowly, his quizzical look turning cold and defensive. It changes everything about his affable, calm self. I see the old Terry, the guy who would have put James McCormick to shame if they'd been competitors.

Still could.

"Who said anything about healing? I'm talking business," Dad scoffs.

Mercifully, the waiter comes to remove our salad plates and

deliver our entrées. Dad prefers to eat quickly these days, then drink leisurely after.

At least he's eating something.

With Dad's mouth busy working a chunk of cow, I take the opportunity to check my phone. Three texts from Shannon making sure I'm okay, and an itemized, triaged list of questions from Dave.

I send Shannon a heart and...

Oops.

That's cute, but the answer is no, Dave texts back.

Sorry, I reply, laughing lightly. *Sent to the wrong person.*

Is this one of those awkward work moments where you expect me to hide an affair you're having? he asks.

No affair. I was sending my heart to Shannon. No need to hide anything, I assure him.

Good. Because if you screw around on your awesome wife, I will help her get a bulldog lawyer and tell the world. Make no mistake where my loyalty lies on that issue, sir.

"How's Shannon?" Dad asks politely. I nearly drop my phone in my garlic mashed potatoes.

"She's, uh, fine." Whatever I look like makes him pay more attention to me than I've experienced in years.

"You sound like a guilty man caught doing something he's not supposed to. Who are you texting with?" Dad cranes to look at my screen. "I see little hearts everywhere."

Terry becomes uncharacteristically nosy and looks, too. "Oh. He's texting his assistant, Dave."

"Dave? Why would you send hearts to him?" Dad asks, then rolls his eyes. "Good God, Declan. There are plenty of attractive women you can have a fling with. Why pick *him?*"

"I am not having an affair with Dave." When did my dad start to sound like Marie?

"If you were, you'd have good taste," Terry teases, which just makes Dad frown deeper, his jowls appearing.

"I wouldn't be the first McCormick to screw his assistant," I say with forced joviality, clapping Dad on the back. "Might even call it a rite of passage."

Dad freezes.

So does Terry.

And then I get it.

Oh, boy, do I get it.

Clearing his throat, Dad turns to Terry. "About that, son..." A long sigh follows.

Then–nothing.

Terry doesn't make it easy.

Eyes jumping wildly all over the table, Dad's clearly searching for some liquid fortitude. None remains, so he defaults to the next option.

Stuffing his face.

Watching my father in a moment of awkwardness, when he doesn't know what to do, is like viewing a nature show where the animal behaves unpredictably, generating breathless excitement from the narrator. I'm not quite certain what I'm watching, but it's potentially dangerous and I can't look away.

Terry leans back in his chair and hails the waiter, who sees Terry's finger-tap on the empty beer pint and removes it, returning two minutes later with a fresh one.

Two minutes during which we watch Dad chew.

I can't take it.

I break first.

"You asked us here to talk about becoming CEO," I say slowly, keeping my voice neutral. Ask it as a question and he may ridicule me; make it a definitive declaration and he could see it as an act of aggression.

"I asked you both here so you can *prove* to me which of you two I should pick," Dad finally says after swallowing, his arm in the air for the server to bring more whisky. For a second, I consider getting another scotch, but it won't help.

So I don't.

"*Prove*," Terry says in that low, firm voice of his, the one I remember from years ago. It could make you feel protected or scare the hell out of you.

Somehow, it elicits both in me.

"I'm not just going to pick one of you and hand it to you," Dad says dismissively. "I did that twice and look where it got me."

Terry gives me a look I don't have words for.

"I suppose Declan feels entitled to it," Dad says with a sniff. "You are, after all, the only son who hasn't been offered the position. Perhaps I should give you your time to shine, after all."

Terry takes a long gulp of his beer and looks at Dad. "When was the last time you talked to Andrew?"

"Who?" Dad says tersely.

"Cut the crap, Dad," Terry says softly. "The silent treatment didn't work with me after Mom died. It doesn't work on Andrew. All it does is reinforce what an unmitigated asshole you can be." His voice is tight and deadly, but his body is loose, stretched back in his seat like he has all the time in the world to cut Dad off at the knees.

There are moments–rare moments–when mastery emerges from people, when we rise above our awkwardness and respond with pitch-perfect eloquence to a need that has arisen. It's like a muscle memory that becomes a state of flow, when our brain wiring integrates with emotions and body.

For Terry, this is such a moment.

And he makes it seem achingly simple.

"I'm the asshole?" We learned the hard way that you lose when you ask a question. Dad realizes it too late.

He's broken his own rule of power dynamics.

Game over.

Terry's the victor.

Except victory comes with a cost, and I'm paying part of that as Dad looks at me and says, "You agree with him?"

"I think the topic is irrelevant," I answer, weaseling out of it while trying to hold my frame.

"You missed your calling, Dec," Terry says, holding his beer glass aloft in a toast to me. "You'd have made a fine politician."

"Too low-stress," I joke, but as the banter continues, I see the confused rage in Dad's eyes.

We're not making the topic irrelevant.

We're making *him* irrelevant.

And he knows it.

That's why he's so desperate.

Ever watch a man deflate before your eyes? It's not a fun sight. There's no joy in it, even when it's a man with an ego the size of a small blimp. Dad's shoulders drop as the light of conquest dims a bit. I would feel sorry for him if I thought it mattered, but it doesn't.

He's been cruel to Andrew because he feels betrayed.

He feels betrayed because he's losing relevance.

He's brought us here in a final attempt to feel like he has some control.

And the deflation is that puffed-up need leaving his body.

"Dad," Terry says gently, using the same tone I would have used if he hadn't spoken first. It's a kind voice.

And our father hates it.

"Stop," Dad warns, slamming his drink to the table with a viciousness the glass doesn't deserve.

"I don't want to be CEO," Terry finishes. He looks at me.

"I don't, either. I have my own company. So does Andrew," I prod.

No reaction.

"And he's recommended several good replacements for himself."

"His judgment is terrible."

Terry's eyebrows shoot up. Aha! Dad acknowledged Andrew's existence.

"Don't say a word," Dad growls, shaking his head. Then he tips his head to the ceiling and mutters, "You were right," to... the sky?

"Damn it, Elena, you were right," he continues, closing his eyes. If he were anyone else, I'd think he was fighting tears.

But he's not anyone else.

"What was Mom right about?" Terry asks gently.

"She said that the goal of parenting wasn't to raise three business powerhouses. It was to raise three strong, independent men. I told her they were one and the same. She laughed and told me independence was a double-edged sword."

Sad eyes, but with a glint of admiration I've never seen before, meet mine, then Terry's. Silence stretches out longer than it should, and Dad suddenly stands.

"The bill's taken care of, boys. See you at Christmas next week, at that godforsaken house in Mendon."

And with that, he leaves, the victory sweet.

Although it sure does leave a bitter taste in my mouth.

Like a whale cleaning out its blowhole, Terry releases all the air in his body from his tense jaw. My own reaction is damn close, though I've learned not to make a sound.

"He hasn't changed," Terry says, turning to me with a wry

expression, shaking his head as he reaches for a glass of mineral water and takes a sip.

"He has. He admitted Mom was right. That's progress."

"Admitting a dead woman was right has no impact on his ego."

"But it's progress." Referring to Mom as *dead woman* makes my skin crawl.

We burst into laughter, the kind survivors share, layered and thick.

"Look at you in a suit."

"Dad told me to be presentable."

I study him as his eyes take in a dessert tray passing by. He waves the server over and we order chocolate mousse cake and lime-strawberry cheesecake.

I'm turning into Shannon.

"Did he ask you to be CEO before this dinner?" Terry inquires, but he knows the answer.

"No."

"Me, either. The guy thrives on competition. I think he gets off on making other people compete, too."

"It definitely fuels him."

"We took the wind out of his sails. Did he seriously think that was going to work?" Terry's question is meant to be rhetorical, but I can hear the emotion under it.

"I think he expected me to jump," I admit, dessert delivered, coffee offered. We both decline and dig into our post-Dad sugar rush.

"Bet you're right. Middle-kid syndrome," Terry says before stuffing his mouth.

"What's that supposed to mean?"

"You're a middle child. You married a middle child. Middle children always crave more attention."

"Now you're a shrink?"

"Dad unfairly blamed you for Mom's death. You'd have made a great CEO of Anterdec. He leapfrogged and picked Andrew, and now our little brother has a backbone, so he left. Dad's floundering. Can't scale up and let his amazing business creation take on a life of its own. He needs to feel like he has control over the person running it, and a non-family member removes that from him."

"He has no choice."

Terry slides his chocolate cake toward me, a gesture that offers me a taste. I shake my head. He spears a piece of my lime-strawberry cheesecake so casually.

Now *he* reminds me of Shannon.

"Dad hates not having the choice."

Troubled eyes meet mine, real and open. "That's right, Dec. And for the first time in James McCormick's life, all three of his kids are telling him no."

We sit in silence.

And then we fist bump.

11

Shannon

Christmas Day

There is an enormous hole in my parents' living room ceiling.

And it is *glowing.*

"DAD?" I scream when I see it, earning a spew of laughter from Amy, who comes downstairs carrying a mug of coffee and a small, wrapped gift with a festive purple bow on top.

"Welcome to Dad's reverse Grand Canyon, holiday edition," Amy says.

"Why is there a hole above the tree?" It's about three feet square, perfectly even, and when I look up, I see rafters, the paper backing of fiberglass insulation, and...

"Is that the star on top of the tree up there?"

"New one. The old one burned in the fire two years ago. This is a big glowing angel."

"*Why?*"

"Because Dad."

"Heya!" Dad booms as he sees me, arms open wide for a bear

hug. His beard's almost entirely grey and white these days, though his auburn hair is still remarkably untouched by age. He smells like woodsmoke and pine tar, with a touch of Old Spice thrown in.

"Dad, why is there a hole in the ceiling?"

"Because the tree didn't fit."

"So you CUT A HOLE IN THE CEILING?"

Amy starts braiding her long auburn hair, shade identical to Dad's, her hip against the dining table, rolling her eyes.

"It was the only way," Dad says with that sigh I know so well, the one that makes him sound like an impatient Bob Vila.

"Why not cut a foot off the bottom of the tree?"

"Already did. Poor Bessie. Can't cut any more off her!"

"But he had no problem destroying the drywall!" Mom shrieks from the kitchen. "And we just had it redone after the fire disaster two years ago!"

"WE AGREED NOT TO TALK ABOUT THAT, MARIE!"

Dad rarely yells, so his touchiness around the Christmas tree, the hole, the Christmas fire–all of it–makes me pull back in wonder.

"Let's focus on this year, Dad," I say soothingly, as if calming an angry gorilla. "What can I do to help?"

"Where are Declan and Ellie?"

"Driving separately."

"Why?"

"Because last year we couldn't fit all the presents in one car."

Right answer. He beams. "Every kid should have such problems."

I can't admit the truth, which is that Declan wants to be able to escape in case there's another disaster.

"Put me to work," I insist, rubbing my hands together. "What can I do?"

"Here," Amy says, handing me a small box.

It's labeled Pet Costumes.

I thrust it back at her, but she's upped her Hot Potato game and Amy isn't stupid.

"Oh, no. I'm not getting stuck with putting the Santa costume on Chuckles again."

"It's Chuckles and Chuffy now," she cackles, running away as I'm left holding the box.

As if summoned, the jingle-jangle of dog tags rings out and little Chuffy appears. A white puffball of goofy goodness, it's not the poor dog's fault Mom gave him a name that means something really different in the UK.

He's a sweet little bichon frise, and he loves having his head scratched.

"Come here," I say, picking him up and giving him what he needs. Chuffy's head pitches back, chin poking up as he yawns with delight, pink tongue lolling out.

He kind of looks like Declan after sex.

"Wook at my Chuffy-Wuffy being wuvved by my widdle giwl," Mom says to us both, the baby talk incredibly annoying. If I ever do that to Ellie, gag me.

Please.

"Want something to drink, Shannon?" Dad calls out from the kitchen. "Declan tells me you like rum and Cokes these days."

"Make it a double, Dad! Mom's doing the baby-talk thing."

"Gotcha!"

"Or just the Coke. No rum," I call out, changing my mind at the last minute.

Snatching the dog out of my arms, Mom does her best "I'm offended" face, which is pretty close to her faces for "Don't you dare try to tell me I'm wrong!" and "What do you mean, my coupon is expired?"

Amy points to the pet costumes box and says to Mom, "I think Shannon is so much better at that, don't you?" in such a sweet voice, she might as well be auditioning for *Annie*.

Ding dong!

I look at the door and see Declan through the glass, standing on the front porch. Ellie is in his arms, thrashing away to get her hands on the wreath.

"Why does he insist on ringing the doorbell, Shannon? Doesn't Declan know he's family? Family just barges in!"

"He has boundaries."

And a deep need never to catch my parents in the middle of sex on the couch again.

"Family doesn't have boundaries," Mom spits out as she stomps across the room. She throws the door open and Ellie pitches into her arms, shrieking, "Gramma! Wanna play with the wreath!"

I look at said wreath. Oh. Right.

It's the peppermint candy wreath Mom made when I was in eighth grade.

"No, sweetie," I tell her. "That candy is old."

"Gramma will get you some new sugar!" Mom chirps as she spins Ellie away from us, taking her into the kitchen, where Mom is about to become my daughter's new best friend and candy pusher.

Dec watches Mom and shakes his head slowly. His arms are impossibly full of bags and presents. How did he carry so much with Ellie in his arms, too?

"Quit ringing the doorbell," I hiss at him as he hands off two bags stuffed with gifts. "Mom doesn't like it."

He flashes me a devilish grin, then gives me a chilled-air kiss on the cheek. "That's why I keep doing it," he whispers in my ear before biting my earlobe.

And then he halts, teeth still clamped down.

"Wha da fook," he says, releasing my ear and staring over my shoulder.

"You're staring at the hole, aren't you?"

"No! You told me it was rude to do that to you in public."

"Dec!" I smack his coated arm hard, earning an ass slap in return. The smile in his moss-green eyes is merry, and I'm filled with an instant warmth as we play off each other. "I meant the hole in the ceiling."

He lets out a long, slow whistle, sounding more like one of Dad's friends as they work on a car together than my billionaire husband.

"That's dedication."

"That's insanity," Amy corrects him.

"You have to admire a guy with a twenty-eight-year-long plan."

"No, you don't!" Amy and I say in unison.

"Who cuts a hole in their ceiling to accommodate a Christmas tree?"

"ME!" Dad bellows as he tickles Amy, who folds like a pill bug and drops to the ground. An instant memory of her as a tiny kid doing that makes me giggle, until oh, no–

I'm the next victim.

Declan takes this as a chance to run back out to the car for round two of gifts, and by the time we stop beating Dad with couch throw pillows and everyone comes to a breathless detente, my husband has somehow arranged the gifts we brought beneath the tree, given Ellie ample attention, scratched Chuffy behind the ears and now Chuckles is purring–*purring!*–contentedly around the cuffs of Declan's business-casual pants.

How can so much American Cool live in one body?

"You could put a nice skylight in there," Declan says to Dad, his hands in his pockets, neck craning around the tree as he looks up. The house reeks of evergreen and pine, Mom's decorating ratcheted up this year. Red velvet bows and silver and white ribbon are interwoven with more greenery than I've ever seen.

It's like we've been dropped into a foam pit at one of those indoor trampoline parks, but instead of foam is Balsam fir branches.

Dad's face brightens. "That's–that's why I did it! Testing it out to see what it would look like."

"Jason, you are so full of hooey," Mom says, Ellie in her arms, my child's face looking like a chocolate disaster zone as she eats an Oreo cookie dipped in chocolate, rolled in candy cane sprinkles, and filled with visions of 3 a.m. hyperactive gymnastics in her big-girl bed tonight. "And by hooey, I mean–"

"Lalalalalalalala," Tyler interrupts. "Don't say a bad word, Grandma!"

Ellie wiggles out of Mom's arms and looks at Tyler in awe as Jeffrey and Carol haul their stuff through the front door, both of them carrying big boxes overflowing with gifts.

"Dad? The au gratin potatoes are in the car, along with the wine. Can you help?"

Dad dutifully slips out the door to shlep.

"There better be your famous peppermint cookies in that car, too," I inform her.

She fixes me with a stare. "Two entire aluminum foil-lined boxes full."

"Great. One for me to take home and one for all of us to share," I say as Carol gasps as she plunks her box down at Declan's feet.

Her eyes meet his. "Do you mind?"

"Do I mind what?" he asks.

"Unloading or getting out of the way."

"How about I get you a drink?"

"I knew you were my favorite brother-in-law."

"I'm your only brother-in-law."

"Not true! Andrew's an honorary one."

"Which means he doesn't count."

She shoos him. "Make yourself useful and get me a drink."

"What do you want? Moscow Mule or beer?"

"Mule."

"Deal."

"Ginger ale is in the wine fridge!" Mom shouts to Declan, who does a double take.

"Wine fridge?" He seems impressed. I'm not going to pop his bubble and tell him the truth. Let him discover it for himself.

"Hey!" I call out to my husband as Ellie does her best imitation of a boa constrictor on my leg. I look down to see that I'm being given chocolate kisses all over my nice white wool pants. "What about me?"

"Your dad's getting you one, right? Or do you want a Moscow Mule, like Carol?"

I make a face. "When have I ever asked for one of those? I want a blueberry-lemon martini." Knowing he can't produce this, I watch him make that long-suffering husband face I know a little too well.

Dad walks past us, boxes in arms, headed straight for the kitchen.

"Then we need to go to a bar. I can manage vodka and ginger ale with lime. What you want requires more than I can handle."

"That's what she said," I mutter out of the corner of my mouth.

Before I realize what's happening, I'm being kissed hard by my laughing husband. It's so good to see him relaxed, happy, joyful, and–*mmmmm*.

His kisses taste better than any–

"CHOCLAT!" Ellie screams as she wiggles between us, one palm on each of our thighs to push us apart. She's entered a new phase called "Daddy Is Mine You Wretched Intruder" whenever Dec and I display any affection toward each other.

Is this her way of making sure she's an only child?

"Mule, or rum and Coke?" Declan asks as he turns Ellie

into a pretzel, her wispy dark hair hanging in a fringe on his shoulder. Upside down and smeared with brown all over her face, she looks like an extra in the *Lord of the Flies* Christmas special.

Dad appears and delivers my glass to me with a wink.

"Virgin," he whispers.

I look around, confused, because there's no way he's talking about me.

Then I realize he means the drink.

"How about a beer?" he asks Declan, who nods. "When Marie and I went back for the van, Perlman gave me a case of some new cinnamon cranberry beer he got from a local guy," Dad says as he rescues us from Ellie's imitation of a crowbar and pulls her up onto his shoulders. Squeals of delight turn to gasps of glee as she looks up at the top of the tree.

"Why dere a hole in the ceiling, Grampa?"

"So the tree will fit."

She looks at me. "Wan a hole in my house."

Dec's eyebrows go up as he walks quickly into the kitchen.

"Get in the hole!" Ellie squeals. Can you tell she watches golf with Declan?

"Cranberry cinnamon is a great scent for soap, Dad. Can't imagine it's any good for beer. I'D LOVE A COFFEE, TOO!" I shout to Declan, who gives me a thumbs up before turning the corner.

"You're not drinking?" Dad's expression makes it clear he's hinting I might be pregnant. "Coke and coffee?"

"I need caffeine for the afternoon. Saving the alcohol unwinding for the Yankee Swap." I rub my palms together.

"Your mother is in it to win it."

"So is Dec."

Ding dong!

Amanda walks in, her head turned behind her, saying to Andrew, "I told you, we don't need to ring the doorbell!"

All hell breaks loose.

It has to.

They have twin toddlers.

Will and Charlie are identical, so bless Amanda for dressing Will in red overalls and Charlie in green. The cuteness quotient is off the charts, so my ovaries, which already do the cha-cha whenever Declan is around, are now ready in full costume for their debut on *Dancing With the Stars*.

Ellie and the twins are fifteen months apart, which makes them adorable together. The boys are nothing but sheer mayhem, while Ellie has the emerging language skills to use them to her advantage.

And all three toddlers worship Tyler.

He beams as he looks at them, like an emperor admiring his people for admiring him.

"Wanna play Jenga?" he asks as Ellie runs to the pile of blocks Tyler's started to dump out of a cloth basket next to the couch, where Mom keeps them. Instantly, Will and Charlie toddle over and begin stuffing them under Chuffy's dog bed.

Amanda's hair is closer to its natural color than I've seen it in a while. "How are you?"

A high, slightly hysterical sound fills the air between us as we embrace. "Oh. You know," she says. "Nannies are off for the holiday and it's just us."

"Just the two of you? With the two of them?"

"Yes. I manage to pee, but don't quite have time to wipe."

"That's TMI."

"*You*, Shannon? *You* are lecturing *me* on bathroom TMI? After you swallowed your engagement ring and we were all on poop watch? No. Just... no."

"I'm sorry," I answer with a laugh. "It's just... wow. You guys have so much going on."

"And work crises for Andrew at both companies."

"Eek. What kind of work crisis does a chain of gyms have?"

"Massive fungal problem in the locker rooms. Health department's involved in two towns. The regional cleaning company Andrew hired turns out to be the subject of a television news investigation on fraud and graft."

I shudder and reach for a plate of buckeyes. "That's a problem that calls for chocolate."

"CHOCLAT!" Ellie screams, abandoning the Jenga blocks for the plate in my hands. Mom happens to come over at that moment, reaching toward Amanda for a hug. She deftly plucks one of the chocolate-peanut butter balls from the plate and palms it off to Ellie on the sly. My daughter handles it all so smoothly, I'm convinced she's a future jewel thief.

Declan's watching Andrew with Will and Charlie, who look like miniature versions of Andrew. It's like my bestie and her husband cloned him and shrunk him down to toddler age. Dec's a little jealous, I think. Not that he doesn't adore Ellie, of course, but I know he'd love a boy.

A boy who looks like him.

Then again, Ellie definitely favors Dec, so if genetic rolls of the dice are fair in any way, shape, or form, our future son should look like me.

"What's the problem at Anterdec?" I ask Amanda, just as the doorbell rings again, and Mom shouts, "James!"

Amanda points to Mom. "*That's* the problem. James."

"You need a drink."

"I need the whole bottle, but I'd prefer coffee right now."

"Coming right up. I know a guy who knows a woman who knows coffee."

Her hug is tighter than usual, and her body has a weird combination of tension and give that says she's tired. Who wouldn't be? Chasing sixteen-month-old twins around with no help while your husband drops the CEO mantle of a Fortune 500 company so he can run his own chain of gyms is... a lot.

Doing it while being iced out by his high-powered billionaire dad is so much worse.

That she just wants a good cup of coffee nearly makes me cry.

Andrew leaves, ostensibly for another load of gifts, but on his way out he has to pass James.

"Hi, Dad."

James completely ignores him.

"Dad. You have to say something to me."

James doesn't even move, waving to Ellie, who gives him a filthy-fisted wave back. My poor kid's blood sugar would make an endocrinologist cringe.

"Dad, would you–"

"James, and Pam!" Mom walks to the doorway and gives Andrew a strange look, but her appearance is enough to make my father-in-law move to give her a polite hug. Pam's eyes comb over the scene, lighting up with merriment at the sight of her grandsons.

Who are currently trying to shove Jenga blocks into Chuffy's ears.

Pam's little teacup chihuahua, Spritzy, shakes in sympathy and clings to Pam.

"OH, NO!" Amy shouts from the kitchen. "Mom? The sour cream's gone bad. What can we use for a substitute?"

Ding dong!

It's a merry-go-round of people.

Terry's the one ringing the doorbell now, Jeffrey finally answering it with, "Why do you ring the doorbell when you can just come in?" Terry says something to him that makes my nephew laugh, then gesture animatedly and offer to carry in a small bag Terry's brought.

Big enough to hold a lot of gift cards, I imagine.

Terry's the only one of the McCormick brothers who isn't married and also the only one who doesn't have kids. He's the single uncle who comes to play, and while Jeffrey and Tyler aren't technically his nephews, he's a kind man who brings presents for all the kids.

"Hey, Dad," he says casually to James, who is now fisting a highball glass and holds it aloft in greeting. It's a far cry from the way James is treating Andrew, and a prickly sensation forms at the base of my spine.

There's always one conflict, isn't there?

Always.

You can't have a big family and expect everyone to get along. When I was little, I was oblivious, not understanding that Dad didn't like someone, or that Mom had been slighted by some relative. We didn't see Mom's mother often, and I later understood why, but Mom and Dad spent so much energy, time, and effort creating as frictionless a life as possible when it came to our little family of five.

I didn't understand how much effort until I married into the McCormick family and saw how they elevate conflict to an Olympic sport.

Complete with medals, gold, silver, and bronze.

Terry gives me a hug, while Jeffrey does his work for him and puts his presents under the tree. As the family expands, so do the number of gifts. It's looking like someone popped a roll of Pillsbury dough, only instead of biscuits, it's presents.

"Dad's here. No Hamish?" Terry asks as I finish hugging him. Amanda sidles over, coffee in hand, and they hug politely. No one's really close to Terry, but I've been in the family longer and know him a wee bit better.

Maybe.

"Why would Hamish be here?" Amanda asks, eyes on the twins, who are currently competing to see who can make Chuffy hide under a pillow better.

"Exactly. Ever notice Dad finds a way to bring him to these gatherings? For a guy who lives in Scotland, he sure does find his way to Boston a lot."

"James uses him," I try to explain.

"What does that mean?"

"Just what I said. It's a very common behavior for aging alpha men. Find a classically attractive, physically fit male specimen and glom onto him on the assumption that there will be transference of the younger man's virility and attractiveness to the aging man."

"He's right behind you," Amanda whispers in my ear.

Oops.

"I–" James, who is overhearing this, turns a fiery shade of red. "That is complete poppycock!"

"No, it's not."

"Where did you learn that theory? Off the back of a Crackerjack box?"

"A what?" Amy asks, perplexed. "What's Crackerjack?"

"Like caramel corn, but with peanuts and a toy prize in the box," Terry explains.

"Like a happy meal for caramel corn?" she asks him, confused.

"Sure. Let's go with that."

Carol shoots Terry a look of camaraderie. "Kids," she mutters.

"Back in our day," he cracks, that deep voice like dark caramel poured over toffee, "we had to wait while we rewound the VHS tape before we could watch a favorite scene over again."

"You had a VCR?" Carol shoots back. "I just had colored pencils and made flip books of Donnie Darko for fun."

"That's one hell of an emo phase," he counters, folding his arms over his chest. The gesture makes his voice seem even deeper, if that's possible. The two share a warm look that makes me glance at Amy.

Who is glancing right back.

Carol and Terry? No way.

And yet... it's not a bad idea, is it?

No. No! Bad idea. Bad, bad idea. It's one thing to end up sisters-in-law with my bestie, but to have my sister also be my sister-in-law? I have no desire to have a family tree that doubles as a Möbius strip.

"Shannon!" Mom calls from the kitchen. "I need you to do the gravy."

Dec looks at me from across the room, where he's barely holding Ellie back from a nine-story Jenga tower. He is somehow protecting it from the desperate destructive attempts of our daughter, who is cartoonishly pinwheeling her arms to knock it down.

"Gravy," I say with a shrug as Ellie gets past him and *bam!*

She's like a C-4 charge in human form.

Will toddles over, picks up a Jenga block, and starts chewing furiously, which makes Ellie and Tyler laugh. Tyler picks up a block and licks it, giggling.

As I leave, I hear Declan shout, "Ellie, that's not a Jenga. That's Chuffy's rawhide bone!"

"Here are the drippings," Mom says, as if I've never seen a roasting pan with all the juices and dark bits from the basting all over the bottom. Making gravy is an art form, and a few years of Mom's lessons have taught me some tricks.

Trick Number 1: Avoid learning for as long as possible and just let your mother make it.

Trick Number 2: Do a terrible job the first year so your Mom takes back over.

Trick Number 3: Mom's "secret spice" is just a blend from Penzey's she gets on sale every year on Black Friday.

Trick number 4: Feign memory loss.

"Mom? How do I do this again? You're *sooooooo* good at making gravy and every time I try, it tastes like paste."

A finger in my face is her answer. "Hah! Don't think that's going to work again, Shannon. I'm on to you. You're a perfectly fine gravy maker. You're not getting out of it this year."

Damn. Worth a try.

I set the tea kettle on for boiling hot water to pour on the pan drippings and find the whisk. Scraping is its own skill, and my forearms are ready.

Mom is wearing an apron that makes her look like her head is the star of a Christmas tree, and she is in her element, moving like she choreographed herself down to the second.

"It's such a small group this year!" she moans.

"Isn't it awful?" Carol chimes in. "Imagine the gall of people, having their own lives and visiting their own families."

"Thank you! I'm glad someone agrees with me, Carol. So far, your father and sisters are telling me I'm ridiculous. All we have today are your father and me, you three girls, Declan, Ellie, Jeffrey, and Tyler." She stops and looks at her nine outstretched fingers. "James. Andrew. Amanda and the twins. Terry. Pam. That's it! Sixteen people!"

"What a ghost town," I reply as the tea kettle whistles. I grab it with one hand, the whisk in the other, and prepare to do battle with turkey fat.

"Are you being sarcastic?" Mom asks, narrowed eyes judging me.

"Me? Nooooooooo."

"Break up those chunks," Mom orders as she watches me.

Ding!

One of the three timers–the oven and two egg timers on the counter–goes off, and Mom mercifully leaves me alone.

Carol is arranging grilled green beans on a platter, Dad now hovering with tongs over a charcoal fire on the patio. He's flipping spears of sweet potato, lips pursed in a whistle.

I remember the hole in the living room ceiling.

"That hole for the tree is crazy," I mutter, expecting Carol to agree, but instead, she winces. My antennae go up.

"What?"

"What what?"

"What's the deal with the tree?"

"Oh, you know. Dad."

"You're not telling me something."

"Mom and Dad never told you?"

"Told me what?"

"About Bessie."

"I know the tree has a name."

"She's twenty-eight years old," Carol says softly. "About ten months older than Amy."

"Ten months? Why are you so specific?" I halt my whisking. "Oh, God. Don't tell me Amy was conceived next to Bessie when she was a sapling?"

"No. But Mom and Dad planted the trees with Pops right after Mom had a miscarriage. Bessie's the last remaining tree."

"Mom had a miscarriage?"

"Yeah. Fourteen or fifteen weeks along."

"Ooof." Declan and I have kept our cards close to our vests and haven't said a word about trying for another baby. A miscarriage is something I know could happen, of course, but I've only thought about it in the abstract.

Hearing about the tree makes it feel so much more real.

"Is that why Dad's being so irrational about Bessie?"

"I think so."

"It's been so long. And they went on to have Amy..." What I'm saying sounds strange, even to my own ears. No one can judge how another person mourns. I should know better.

"They did. And it's not like they dwell on it. But Pops died this year, and Bessie's the last tree, so..."

"I had no idea."

"I figured. Don't say anything to them tonight."

"I won't." Making fun of the tree takes on a subtext I hadn't considered before, filling me with misplaced guilt.

Ding!

Just as another buzzer goes off, Declan walks into the kitchen and looks at what I'm doing.

"That's how you make gravy?"

I hold up the whisk, eager to shift emotional states, my husband making it nice and easy suddenly. "Want to learn?"

"No."

"JASON! THE HAM!" Mom pulls a large roast out of the oven. It has the power to summon James, who walks in and looks at the beef.

"Why, Marie! I didn't know you had it in you."

"Had what in me?"

"The ability to handle a fine cut of meat like that."

Dad walks in the kitchen carrying the smoked ham and says,

"She's been married to me for more than three decades, James. She can handle plenty of fine meat."

James rolls his eyes, but laughs as Mom blushes. Andrew offers Dad a clap on the back and says, "Good one."

James goes stone faced and walks away, the tension clear.

"Still not talking to you?" I ask Andrew, whose ankle is suddenly assaulted by a little blond cherubic being he helped to create.

One who sits on his foot and starts babbling "Dadadadadadadadadadada."

"At least someone recognizes my existence," he murmurs, smiling brightly at Charlie as he lifts him up off the ground into his arms. Charlie rewards his dad for the shower of attention by shoving one fat little finger straight up Andrew's right nostril.

"James will thaw," Carol says carefully as Terry wanders in, hovering at the periphery, followed by a curious Jeffrey.

Whose curiosity is focused entirely on caloric consumption. He's grown so much this year, he's getting closer to my height, and I'm a tall woman. He snags a big dinner roll and a handful of cashews and disappears.

"Thaw? Dad?" Terry says, sharing a look with Andrew and Declan that makes my heart hurt.

"He can't ignore you forever," I pipe up.

McCormick men have a tone, a unique sound that comes from the back of their throats when they don't believe something you've said.

I've never heard it in triplicate before.

The gravy is close to ready, my work with arrowroot powder succeeding as I use a sifter to slowly sprinkle it. Pam's fighting Lyme disease and has dietary restrictions, so we use this as a thickener now, and Mom swears it tastes the same.

Ding!

Dad comes back in the kitchen triple-loaded, with Ellie under one arm, Will under another, and Tyler on his back.

"I need the oven to cook some children!"

Tyler drops off with an ear-piercing shriek.

"NO! NO, GRANDPA! THAT WOULD HURT A LOT!"

"Dad," Carol chides, racing to Tyler's side, whispering in his ear. Tyler nods slowly as Jason gently drops Ellie and Will,

Andrew grabbing his son and hoisting both boys like sacks of potatoes.

Whatever Carol's saying to Tyler is helping, his eyes cutting to the oven.

Finally, he says, "The oven is off. Grandpa can't cook Ellie and Will. Grandpa?"

"Yeah, buddy?"

"What temperature do you cook children?"

"DINNER!" Mom shouts as she grabs the big roasting pan from me, pours the gravy into two big boats, and glides into the dining room to set them on the long table with seats for "only" sixteen.

I take my seat, Ellie between Declan and me, her high chair pushed up against the table.

"Whew!" Mom says, looking at the clock. "4:03. Best time ever! Only three minutes late."

"And no one's set the tree on fire," Amy adds. "Yet."

Everyone glares at her.

Even the twins.

And then we feast.

12

Declan

The Yankee Swap, a.k.a Dirty Santa

"Kids are settled," I announce softly as I find a spot on the sofa next to my wife and put my arm around her shoulders. The feel of a steady adult who stays in place for more than half a second is a welcome change from managing Ellie.

"You mean Will, Charlie, Ellie, and Tyler are," Jeffrey says smugly. He's flexing his not-kid muscles with the condescension of a thirteen-year-old who knows damn well one cocked eyebrow from Grandma or Grandpa can drop him back down into kid class, but he can't help himself.

Amanda comes out of the hallway, Andrew at her heels, the two of them positively giddy.

"We got the twins down! They're both asleep at the same time," Amanda whispers as if she's invented teleportation.

"It's a Festivus miracle!" Andrew crows. He grabs Amanda's hand and whispers something in her ear. She turns beet red and her eyes go shifty.

I know that look.

Shannon picks that exact moment to catch what's going on, then gaze at me like it's contagious.

Because the look my brother gave his wife is the look of a new father trying to get some nooky while the babies are asleep. Those rare, stolen moments when two minutes is all you need.

Sometimes just two strokes. Not that I'd know about that.

A raspy, furtive series of whispers bounces between Andrew and Amanda as a negotiation worthy of the Paris Peace Talks takes place. I sympathize. Who wants to have a quickie on Christmas in someone else's house?

Andrew.

Andrew does.

"It's like being an anthropologist studying the mating habits of the slightly less interesting brother in a family," I say out of the corner of my mouth.

"I heard that!" Andrew snaps. "You must be looking in a mirror, bro."

Shannon suddenly feels so good against me, her soft curves begging to be touched, her little sighs of contentment making me imagine whimpers and pleas.

Frustration Nooky is suddenly on the table.

See what I mean? Contagious.

"No," she hisses as she realizes what's happening, her voice meant to cut this idea off at the knees. "Just because they have twins and are desperate to hump like bunnies on the floor of a locked bathroom with a dog bed for a cushion doesn't mean I am!"

"But there *is* a cushion."

"DECLAN!"

The rapid-fire murmurs between Andrew and Amanda are killing me. Sex talk is a contagion. Knowing my brother is about to bust one with his wife and I'm not isn't an aphrodisiac in and of itself, of course.

But knowing he's getting off–and I'm not–makes me *think*.

And not with my brain.

Amanda whispers the word *bathroom*, then the word *basement*, and Shannon scooches away from me, reaching for a big chunk of chocolate peppermint bark that is her version of foreplay for sex we're not having.

Not having.

"If you want something sweet, I've got a candy cane for you," I whisper in her ear, earning a groan of disgust.

"When did you become 'that husband'?"

When she pulls out the finger quotes, I know I'm in trouble.

"What's 'that husband' mean?" I ask as I watch Andrew grab Amanda's hand and lead her to a place it looks like I won't be visiting.

The place where you have sex with your wife.

"Just because Andrew and Amanda are playing Two Minutes in the Basement doesn't mean we have to follow suit. If Andrew jumped off a cliff, would you follow?"

"Is there sex at the bottom of that cliff? Then yes."

"Declan!" Marie squeals, walking over with two steaming hot mugs. Cinnamon and cloves waft up. "Here's your hot toddy!"

Carol snorts. "I hate that a drink so good has to be tainted by such an awful name."

Terry's sitting in a chair next to her, his frown of confusion making me realize just how little he knows about my in-laws. "What's wrong with hot toddy?"

"My ex-husband's name is Todd."

"He's the worst dad ever," Jeffrey contributes, finding his entry point. The kid is hovering quietly, with the energy of an overeager puppy two seconds away from peeing all over the kitchen floor in excitement over getting a special treat.

"Jeffrey," Jason says softly, but it's less a chiding tone and more plaintive. Dad looks at us uncomfortably and reaches for one of Marie's gingerbread cookies.

Being treated like an adult by staying up with the rest of us emboldens the kid, who looks to Carol and says, "You always say that, though." He tilts his head, brow dropping, and I can see the man he'll be one day. He looks so earnest, trying hard to find meaning in a world he's exploring.

And seeking a place to land.

"Sounds like we need a new name for the drink," Terry declares, deftly avoiding conflict, which is his superpower. "How about Warm Apple Pie?"

"Or Loose Lips," Dad says, which makes Terry laugh.

"Feeling good, Dad?" he asks, giving our father a big grin, the interplay between them making my breath catch. This is rare.

So rare, I can't remember a moment like this since our mother died.

Dad looks at Pam, who is smiling back. "Feeling fine."

Andrew and Amanda return, literally like clockwork: Two and a half minutes have passed. Amanda's face is flushed and Andrew looks like he made a hole in one.

"Two-pump chump," I whisper as Andrew leans across me to grab a sugar cookie.

"Envy's never been a good look on you," he lobs back as Shannon and Amanda play some non-verbal game with their eyes and cheek muscles that involves stuffing their faces with sweets and pretending no one notices the kinetic semaphore they're conducting.

When I met Shannon, I would have dismissed them as silly and superficial. Just say what you're thinking.

Now I know it's part of decades of hardwiring, a kind of subculture that has depth.

It's still annoying, though.

"I can't believe how many presents the kids got," Shannon finally says, looking around the room with a breathless joy that makes my heart seize. "I'm glad we brought two cars, because we had to put some of Will and Charlie's presents in ours!"

"Next year, we're bringing a dump truck," Andrew jokes as he winks at Amanda, who maintains eye contact for just long enough to make me stroke Shannon's knee.

Another body part of mine seizes now, but it'll have to wait.

Jason waves to me from the kitchen, and I reluctantly abandon skin contact with my warm, soft wife and follow him into the laundry area of their house, where he points and says, "I finished the frame for you."

It's the stained glass. Dogs playing poker.

Kilty.

When I bought it, one corner was slightly broken. Tillie warned me it needed to be properly framed, and Marie came home and mentioned it to Jason, who texted me to offer.

One of the strangest aspects of being in the Jacoby family is how someone always offers to help with a problem you haven't even mentioned. Intuitively, they notice.

They offer.

And then they act.

It's a fine character trait in an employee. In a family member, though, it's alien to me.

Or, at least, it was–until I married Shannon.

"This is beautiful, Jason. Solid craftsmanship." He took the stained-glass window and added a narrow metal frame to it. The metal holds the piece securely together, and he added a chain for hanging.

"Thank you." His hand lands on my shoulder, connecting us, and in the act, connecting him to my mother, too. "I have to say, I laugh every time I look at that." Chuckling, he reaches for a large red plastic bag printed to look like a wrapped present. "And here you go. I'm sure he'll like it."

"I hope so."

"You certain you want to give it away? It has a lot of meaning for you."

"It means even more to him."

A squeeze on the shoulder and we're done, Jason helping me to put the frame in the bag, the drawstring simple.

We walk back into the living room. Carol and Terry are still in chairs next to each other, Jeffrey between them, cross-legged on the ground, plowing his way through a cheese tray with a side of chocolate truffles. Carol and Terry sip their hot toddies–or should we call them Loose Lips?

Dad and Pam are on the loveseat. Shannon, Amanda, and Andrew are on the big sofa, with plenty of room for me next to my wife. Jason brought in dining room chairs for Marie, Amy, and himself.

We are twelve.

"Twelve days of Christmas!" Marie calls out, pointing as she counts.

Dad groans. "I thought we were done singing."

Andrew keeps glancing at Dad. I walk over to him and announce, "It turns out there's one more present." I hand the big bag to him, leaving the space on the sofa empty so he has room to move.

"What's this?" he asks. "We already exchanged gifts."

"It's something special."

"You can't do this! Now I have to find another gift for you so we're even."

"Not everything has to be a competition," Jason declares quietly.

Dad, Andrew, and I snort.

Terry shakes his head slowly as Carol leans toward him and whispers, "You got a different set of genes, didn't you?"

"Nah. I just got out at a younger age."

"Good for you."

They share a smile, Carol's eyebrows up, one corner of her mouth curled in a conspirator's smile as she brings the hot drink to her lips and looks away.

Terry points to Andrew's gift. "Open it!"

Andrew does.

And instantly turns into a seven-year-old boy.

"Kilty." The word comes out in an awed hush, Amanda leaning against him to look at the design.

"Dogs playing poker!" Amanda says joyfully, laughing hard.

But Andrew doesn't laugh.

"Kilty?" Dad says to him, making everyone jump, because finally–*finally!*–Dad's ended seven months of silence.

And all it took was Mom. Even in death, Elena Montgomery McCormick finds a way.

"Look," Andrew says, turning the frame. Dad's eyes widen, nose twitching with a smile.

"Sure does look like him. That damn dog was the bane of my existence. We finally let him sleep in your bed because he wouldn't let me sleep in mine!" Dad's jovial explanation makes everyone do a double take.

"What do you mean, James?" Pam asks.

"Kilty took to Elena like he imprinted on her. Which, I suppose, he did. Elena was a softy for kids and animals, and when we attended a humane society fundraiser, she heard about a mother dog who had just died, leaving four pups. Kilty was one of them. Brought him home at around six weeks. By the time he was three months old, he was territorial. Nothing I did made that damn dog understand *I* was top dog."

Everyone's listening intently, even Jeffrey.

"For more than a year, Kilty would sleep next to Elena in our bed. Nothing I said made a difference. If we locked the dog out of the room, he whimpered and scratched."

"I know!" Andrew replies. "I kept getting him and bringing him into my room."

"That dog drove me out of my own bed. It was a lean year," Dad adds with a wink and a scowl, somehow pulling off the combination.

"What do you mean?" innocent Jeffrey asks.

Carol shushes him.

"You started taking him in your room more and more. You couldn't have been more than seven," Dad adds, looking at Jeffrey. "And Terry was about your age, Declan in the middle."

"Turn the frame over, Andrew," I say gently, fighting emotion.

He does.

And his mouth tightens, throat jumping as he struggles.

Fingertips on the words that show it really is Kilty, Andrew traces, breathing in slowly through his nose to control himself.

"Mom," he finally says, looking at me. "Mom made this."

Dad's on his feet in an instant. "She what?"

"I found it at a flea market," I begin to explain, Andrew giving me a puzzled look.

"What is a flea market? Why would you go somewhere that sells insects?"

Aggrieved sighs pour out of Dad and Terry.

"I sure sheltered you, didn't I?" Dad intones as he stands next to Andrew. Amanda whispers something to Shannon about the silent treatment ending.

Let's hope.

"A flea market is a place where people sell used stuff. There was a woman, Tillie Ehrenright, selling stained glass from her father's studio in Weston, and one thing led to another," I start to explain.

"Ehrenright?" Dad's eyebrows lift as he blinks hard, a small smile tickling his lips. "Haven't heard that name in forever. Elena loved his little hippie art studio. Went there with a group of hens. She said it was more about wine than art." His gaze jumps to the glass pane with Kilty on it.

"I was right," Marie ventures, looking smug. "I told Declan to stop being such a snob about going to my secret Yankee Swap gift place, but–"

"I thought St. Bonaventure's was the secret place," Carol says.

Shannon turns to her. "No–Funicularelli's is!"

"Marie," Jason adds, "You told me it was In the Doghouse, the thrift shop for the animal rescue place."

"Grandma told me it was the Trash and Treasure shack at the town transfer station!" Jeffrey protests.

We all look at her.

She waves her hand dismissively, moving next to James and gushing, "Look at little Kilty! And the one in the right corner looks like my Chuffy!"

Who is in Pam's lap, hogging Spritzy's place.

Spritzy's in Chuffy's dog bed by the fire, snoring gently.

"Here," Andrew says suddenly, thrusting the framed glass at James. "You have it." Our eyes meet.

I don't have to nod.

I get it.

"Declan gave that to you," Dad says firmly, pushing it back.

"And I'm giving it to you. Kilty meant a lot to me, Dad, but this is a piece of Mom no one knew was out there. Let me give it to you."

"Son," Dad says with a long sigh. "You have the estate in Weston. That's where Kilty lived his whole life. It's where your mother's presence is strongest. This should have a place of honor in the house." He frowns at it. "Even if it is vulgar and god-awful."

"I think it's hilarious!" Marie argues.

"You would."

"Dad." Andrew turns to him, facing him head on. "It's good to be seen again."

Discomfort washes over the room.

"I'm sure it is," Dad says tightly. "Everyone wants to be seen."

And that's the closest anyone's getting to an apology.

"Yankee Swap!" Marie calls out, trying to diffuse the tension. Amy reaches for a small bowl with little pieces of paper in it, folded up.

"You all know how this works?"

Everyone but Dad, Andrew, and me nods yes.

Terry laughs. "You're never done a Yankee Swap? A.k.a Dirty Santa, a.k.a White Elephant?"

"I've watched," I inform him.

"But I never paid attention to the rules," Andrew adds.

"Number one is the best one to get," Marie begins.

Dad, Andrew, and I sit up straight.

"Because you go last."

"That makes no sense," Dad blusters as Pam shushes him.

"Number one looks at all twelve presents and picks one. Opens it. And then holds it. Number two takes a present, opens it, then has a choice: keep it, or take the present away from number one."

"And it goes down the line until number one gets their turn to take whichever present they want from the opened gifts?" Dad asks, for clarity.

"You catch on fast, James!" Marie compliments him.

Dad just rolls his eyes.

And the bowl is passed around.

We each take a piece of paper and open it slowly. Jeffrey's poker face is so terrible, it's clear he pulled number two, which is the worst position to have in any game like this.

I am eleven. Not bad.

"What'd you get?" Shannon asks me. I show her. She holds her paper out.

Seven.

A Cheshire Cat grin forms on Terry's face as he reads his number.

Dad looks pissed.

Andrew and Amanda are huddled together like they're planning how to bang one out in the pantry closet.

"Number one?" Marie calls out, acting like Vanna White as she runs her fingertips through the air over the motley collection of Yankee Swap gifts on the coffee table.

"Me!" Amy says, jumping up and perusing the options. A round thing that rattles when she shakes it, haphazardly taped like a kid did it, is the one she picks.

"That's mine!" Jeffrey announces, to no one's surprise.

Tearing at it with abandon, she reveals a coffee can. A plain, boring coffee can. As she peels the plastic lid off, she bursts out laughing.

It's full of all the Halloween candy a teenager would hate.

"Lollipops! Coconut chocolates! Chewies!" she shouts,

pouring the whole thing on the floor before scooping it back up. "There must be five pounds in here."

"And three grand in dental work," Jason mutters. "Those caramels will yank a crown in three seconds flat. Ask me how."

"I guess I'm keeping this for now," Amy laughs, fist bumping Jeffrey. "Who's number two?"

"Me!" Jeffrey says, grabbing a small, flat package. "I wonder what's in here." As he unwraps it, Amy starts to giggle.

"I assume you brought that one?" Dad says to her, which shuts her up instantly.

"It's a mousepad?" Jeffrey's voice goes up in a question at the end, then he turns sheepishly weird.

"Show us!" Marie insists.

He does.

In bold letters on the front, it says: CUM.

In tiny letters below: Computer User Management.

"Swag for the win," Carol whispers as Terry glances at Jeffrey, clearly wondering if this is okay.

"Amy!" Marie gasps. "That's so vulgar."

"I know!"

"I love it! Jason, when it's your turn, get it."

"Marie, I'll make my own decisions."

She just smiles at him.

Jeffrey looks at Amy's coffee can and trades.

"No fair!"

Jason looks in the can. "Blech. It's all the bad candy!"

"That's the point, Grandpa," Jeffrey says with a pout. "Bad candy's better than a mousepad covered with... that."

Amy winces, and Shannon calls out, "Three?"

Carol walks to the gift table and plucks a beautifully wrapped gift, a shirt box covered in red satin paper with a cream bow. She sits and opens it.

And bursts into uncontrolled laughter.

"What is it, Mom?" Jeffrey asks, wiggling next to her, pulling a t-shirt out of the box.

"It's–oh, my God," Carol gasps. "Who brought this?"

Terry's smirk reveals the answer.

Jeffrey holds up a ratty t-shirt from a Backstreet Boys concert.

Amanda and Shannon gasp, then begin squealing like animals being sent to slaughter.

"I want that!" Amanda calls.

"'I want it that way,'" Shannon says, then hums a tune that makes me groan in disgust.

"Where did you get this?" Carol presses Terry, who laughs.

"Old girlfriend. I was searching my closet to find something to bring for tonight and it was in a crushed box. Thought it would be funny to bring it here and have it be the gift no one wanted."

"I WANT IT!" Amanda, Carol, and Shannon all scream in unison.

Carol hugs it to her chest. "Mine! It's mine! You two have to wait your turns." She nudges Jeffrey. "And if one of them steals it, you steal it back with your turn."

"Mo-OM!" he whines. "First of all, I already went. How much alcohol have you consumed?"

Carol snorts. "Enough to forget that you already went."

He takes a deep breath, ready to lecture her. "And second of all, I get my own turn. We're separate economic actors in this simulation of game theory."

"Everyone hold up their presents so Carol can see!" Marie orders, interrupting the teen.

Jeffrey holds up his coffee can of candy.

Amy holds up her own mousepad.

Carol holds up the t-shirt and declares, "I'm not trading."

"Number four?" Marie calls.

Dad stands up and looks at the three items, deeply bewildered. "I take one of these wrapped gifts, yes?" He gestures toward the table.

"Yep!" Jeffrey answers him.

A large rectangular box, expertly wrapped, is the one Dad picks. I stifle a snicker as Jason winks at me.

Taking his time, Dad moves slowly, winking at a frustrated Jeffrey as he finally opens the box and pulls out a neon–

"What on Earth is this contraption?" he asks as he clutches the rounded edge of a ThighMaster. "Is this a doorstop?"

Pam giggles as Spritzy jumps in her lap, demanding ear scratches. "I haven't seen one of those in decades."

"What is it?" Jeffrey asks. "Is it a marital aid?"

"JEFFREY!" nearly every adult in the room booms at once.

"What?" He lets out a puff of condescension. "I thought

there would be sex stuff! This grown-up Yankee Swap game is way more boring than I thought it would be!"

Terry elbows him. "Do you even know what a marital aid is?"

Uncertainty floods the poor kid's face. "I know Grandma talks about them too much and Auntie Shannon always tells her to cut it out. Mom, too."

"MOVING ON," Jason shouts, looking at Dad. "James, you can keep your ThighMaster, or trade it for the coffee can of candy, the Backstreet Boys t-shirt, or the mousepad."

"This is the strangest set of presents I have ever seen," Dad begins. He grabs both rounded ends of the ThighMaster and presses inward, face lighting up with recognition. "Oh! I see. It's like Charles Atlas. This is for strengthening your pecs!"

"It's for strengthening something that begins with P, yes," Marie begins before Jason pops a buckeye candy in her mouth to shut her up.

"Five!" Carol calls out.

Amanda stands, picks a tiny green box taped to a larger cylinder, and sits back down, peeling the smaller box off the taller gift.

"Oooo, that's mine!" Carol says as Amanda shakes the little green box. It makes a rattling sound.

Amanda opens it to reveal a jar of silvery, sparkly vitamins.

"Vitamins?"

"They're supposed to be specially formulated for stressed-out mothers who need a break."

"Okay," Amanda says.

"And they make your poop glitter."

Marie perks up.

Amanda turns to the tall, cylindrical present that must be a liquor bottle. Now Dad's paying strong attention to the game.

Upon opening it, though...

"Oh, boy." It's a package of 100 glow sticks.

"OOOOOO!" Jeffrey exclaims, then shifts back to cool teenager mode.

"Want to trade?" Amanda offers.

Jeffrey shakes his head. "I don't need vitamins for women. I want to keep my testosterone."

Standing, Amanda says, "Hold those presents up! I'm trading!"

Carol's face falls. "What? You don't like them?" Her fake pout makes Terry laugh.

Reaching for the ThighMaster, Amanda hands the vitamins and glowsticks to a deeply confused Dad, who sets them down like they're a jar full of tarantulas.

"Six!"

Pam's turn. She chooses my gift, a six-foot long box that looks like it might have a pair of skis in it.

"This weighs a ton!" she exclaims. "What could be in there?"

Shannon nudges me. "Ask him."

"This is yours?" Pam asks, laughing as Spritzy begins nosing at the box.

"Mmm hmm."

"Spritzy certainly likes it!" The teacup Chihuahua is now biting one corner.

As Dad peels the dog off the box, Pam begins to open it, the top easy to remove once the ribbon's undone.

She bursts into laughter as Spritzy escapes Dad's arms and attacks the item.

"Is that a six-foot-long rawhide bone?" Terry asks, groaning.

"Complete with a layer of real oxtail," I gloat.

"Dave bought that for you, didn't he?" Shannon hisses at me.

Spritzy is practically humping the thing.

"I don't think this will even fit in my Mini Cooper!" Pam protests, standing and walking to Jeffrey, hand held out. "I want the bad candy."

"Pam!" he squeals. "We don't have a dog. Mom won't let us." He glares at Carol.

Chuffy notices the rawhide bone and comes over, tail wagging, as Spritzy bares his teeth at the competition.

"Awww," Amanda says, beaming at Andrew. "They look like you and Declan when you're having a contest."

"I am far cuter," Andrew notes calmly, as if it's a point of fact.

As I open my mouth to argue, Shannon buckeye bombs me.

Family coping strategy.

"Well, Jeffrey," Pam says, taking the coffee can anyway, "it turns out I love all the candy in here, and maybe having that enormous bone will make your mom rethink the dog issue. You'd never have to buy any treats."

"Thanks, Pam. Appreciate it," Carol says drolly, making Terry laugh.

"Seven!" Amanda calls as Shannon stands.

"Me!" My wife looks over the remaining six presents, all different sizes and shapes. Dad's whispering in Pam's ear and she seems to be patiently explaining something to him. He's still frowning, though.

Jason winks at me. "Good luck, son."

"It's my turn," Shannon informs me, reaching for something that makes Andrew smirk.

Wonder what Gina bought for him to bring?

She opens the small box and holds up... underwear.

Men's underwear.

"The Marriage Saver," she reads aloud from the label. "With special carbon filters to make your man smell like a rose, even in repose."

The room erupts into laughter.

"No way am I trading with Auntie Shannon now!" Jeffrey announces.

"Hey, Pam!" Shannon says, wiggling the underwear. "Trade you!"

"Why would you want a coffee can filled with crappy candy?" I protest.

"It's not your choice!" my wife informs me. "Jeffrey won't trade now."

"Good. We won't get stuck with that thing." I point to the rawhide bone.

"You mean the thing *you* brought?"

"Don't blame me. Blame your mom. She's the one who told me to buy it at the flea market."

"You mean Dave didn't buy it for you?"

"Nope."

She kisses my cheek. "You're growing, Declan. It's so touching to watch. Buying your own dog bones and everything." Shannon hands Pam the underwear and returns to the couch next to me.

"How about I put you in charge of my bone?" I whisper in her ear, earning a thigh smack and an eye roll.

"Eight!" Amanda calls out in the middle of a yawn. "Let's move faster. The twins might wake up."

"That's what she said," Andrew quips, getting his own thigh smacked, but from a laughing wife.

He leaves the room and returns with two cups of coffee, hers with cream. She grins at him. I look at Shannon, who arches one eyebrow and whispers, "If you're going to compete with Andrew, why not compete in the 'wait on your wife' contest?"

"He's already number one at being whipped."

"Declan!"

"I'm number eight," Jason announces.

A large silver box with a red bow and silver bells attached, professionally wrapped, has been on the floor next to the coffee table the entire time. He goes for it.

Dad winks at me.

Ah. Got it. That's whatever Dad's assistant got. Bet he forwarded her the email Marie sent out and has no idea what's in there.

Shaking the box, Jason makes a production of moving slowly, a comedic performance that has everyone laughing before he finally opens the box, Amy next to him.

Her gasp sounds like a train whistle.

"What is this?" Jason asks as he pulls out a woman's purse, the big kind Shannon and her mother carry for everyday use. This one is dark brown with a tan repeat pattern on it and a tan handle.

"IS THAT A REAL VUITTON BAG?" Marie screeches, wrenching it out of Jason's hands before the poor man can blink.

But Amy's holding one of the straps.

Pam turns to Dad. "That's a Louis Vuitton bag, James!"

"Yes. Is there something wrong with it? The directions said to bring something fun."

"We're lucky he didn't bring a twenty-year-old Anterdec intern with a secret piercing and a forked-tongue body mod, wrapped in a bow."

"I would never bring someone like that!"

"Good."

"Because who would give *that* away?" Dad chuckles.

"If it's real, that's a two-thousand-dollar purse!" Carol chokes out.

Everyone looks at Dad, who looks back, just as confused.

"Yes. Of course, it's real. Why on earth would I bring a fake... anything?"

"James," Pam says patiently. "The Yankee Swap rules clearly state that the item has to be used, or have a value of under twenty dollars."

"Twenty dollars! Surely you're joking! I told my assistant that was a typo."

"What was a typo?" Jason asks with a sigh.

"The decimal point. She asked when it said two-zero-point-zero zero and I told her that had to be an error. Who can buy anything of value for twenty dollars?"

"I can!" say Jeffrey, Marie, Jason, Amy, and Carol, all at once.

"Jason, you keep that bag!" Marie insists. "I've always wanted a real one."

I turn to Shannon. "Why didn't we get her one for Christmas?"

"Because we have dollar limits for what we spend on each other."

"She's going to get the purse because of Dad's error."

"Remember?" Amy says, waving her piece of paper. "I'm number one!"

Competition isn't just a McCormick trait after all.

Eyes narrowing with a cunning I haven't seen since our crazy wedding, Marie looks at her own youngest child like she's a fellow contestant on *Survivor*.

"NINE!" Shannon and Carol shout at the same time, trying to distract.

"That's me," Andrew says, standing and reaching for one of the four remaining presents as Amy gloats with anticipatory victory and Marie calculates her chances of getting that bag.

Zero, Marie.

They're zero.

But I'm not going to state the obvious.

Andrew selects a slim envelope, opens it, and pulls out a gift card with a very familiar logo that instantly makes me bare my teeth.

"It's a gift card for Starbucks," he says, holding it up, then shaking a foil card out of the envelope. "And a weird ticket?"

"A scratch ticket!" Jeffrey shouts. "Ooooo!"

"What's a scratch ticket?" I ask, leaning in.

I'm rewarded with raised eyebrows from all of the Jacoby family and Pam. "You don't know what a scratch ticket is?" Jeffrey asks, agog.

"No," Andrew and I say as Terry shakes his head again and sighs.

"You two are as cloistered as nuns," he mutters, reaching for a handful of maple cashews.

"It's a lottery ticket," Jeffrey gushes. "You take a coin and scratch the stuff off the boxes and see if you win."

Shannon's hand goes to my knee as she says with over-enunciated patience, "It's like playing bingo."

Andrew and I brighten. "Oh!"

"Only you can win money."

"Even better!" Andrew says, looking at the six-foot rawhide bone Chuffy's now practically humping. It's Jeffrey's gift now and I know what my brother is thinking.

Whether he'll do the right thing is another question.

"The Starbucks card has sixteen cents on it," Amanda adds, laughing. "And there are two scratch tickets in there."

Andrew fishes around in the envelope and produces the second one. "So there are." Extending the envelope, he offers it to Jeffrey, who beams.

"Andrew!" Amanda groans. "Where are we going to fit a six-foot rawhide bone in the car?"

"We're not," he says out of the corner of his mouth. "We'll conveniently forget it when we leave. The chaos of the twins will be more than enough cover."

"Smart."

He kisses her cheek and winks at me.

"TEN!" Jeffrey shouts.

"That's me," Terry rumbles, standing and going to the meager pickings at the table, "Ten drummers drumming," he adds, half singing in that *basso profundo* voice of his. He's a walking subwoofer.

"What am I supposed to do with this?" James asks Pam as he holds up his bottle of vitamins and glow sticks. "No one has traded for it."

"We have four more chances, James. You never know!" She pats her charcoal-filter underwear.

Terry picks up a box wrapped in snowflake paper, no more

than a foot tall, with a white bow. He tears off the paper to reveal a plain brown box.

Inside the box is a chicken. A yellow plastic chicken.

"What is this?"

"It looks like a lamp," Amy offers.

Terry examines it. "There's no way to turn it on."

"Plug it in," she suggests. Terry does, but still can't find a switch.

"Here," Marie chimes in, reaching for the chicken's neck. "You have to squeeze and slide up." Doing so, she turns the warm, dim light on.

"You have to choke the chicken to light the lamp?" Terry asks, folding in half with laughter.

"Everyone hold up your gifts in case Terry wants to trade!" Marie says, then turns to Jason. "Except you. Hide that purse!"

"Nope. I'm keeping my chicken-choker lamp," Terry announces, hugging the damn thing.

"My turn," I announce before someone shouts my number. I grab the closest present.

Pam smirks.

Once I open it, I understand why. It's a jar of grey goo.

"What is this?" It's unmarked. I hold it up to the light, looking for something that identifies it.

"It's from your Anterdec spa in Las Vegas. A client at my firm is a competitor, and they use that in their spas as well. We were doing a risk analysis on that product, so I got a free sample. It seemed like the perfect Yankee Swap gift."

"But what is it?" Dad asks as Marie holds her hand out to me in a movement that says, *May I?*

I hand it to her. She opens it and sniffs, then pulls her neck back in disgust.

"That smells like jizz. How many men did you–"

"MOM!" Carol shouts, looking at Jeffrey.

"It is semen," Pam explains patiently. "But it's not human."

Amanda starts giggling.

"It's what makes the ocean salty," she says, slapping Shannon's knee, the two completely losing it as Pam smiles wider, Marie looks even more confused, and the rest of us just try not to smell the jar.

"Pamela, what is it?" Dad bluntly asks.

"Whale semen," she says as Dad nods sagely, stopping abruptly when the meaning of her words hits him.

"Whale–"

"JIZZ!" Marie gasps. "The spa! Lüq! Is it really that salty?" One finger flexes, and she's about to dip it in.

"The one you touch is the one you take," Shannon informs her, using a phrase from Ellie's teacher at Mommy and Me playgroup. Marie freezes, then carefully screws the lid on and hands it back to me.

"Trade!" I call out. "Hold your presents up high, because I am trading."

Panic floods Marie's face as she looks at Jason, who is holding the Vuitton bag.

Amy holds up her mousepad.

Jeffrey holds up the Starbucks card and scratch tickets.

Carol hugs her Backstreet Boys t-shirt.

Dad points to his vitamins and glowsticks and shakes his head.

Amanda squeezes the ThighMaster.

Shannon points to the coffee can of candy.

Marie sits in Jason's lap suddenly, hiding the Vuitton bag.

Andrew lazily points to the rawhide bone I brought.

Terry chokes his chicken... lamp.

I hand Andrew the whale sperm and stare at the bone.

"You're such a jerk," he mutters as we trade.

"I think what you're trying to say is 'You won, Declan.'"

"Last one's for you, Mom," Carol notes, looking at Amy, who is staring at Marie's ass.

"Jason can just take it and open it. I want the Vuitton bag."

"And then just hand it to me," Amy calls out. "Because it's mine."

"That's not fair!" Marie complains.

Dad yawns. "Was that it? This is the last one?"

Jason extracts the bag from under Marie's butt, Marie blocking him like an aggressive forward in an NBA game.

But Amy's nimbler.

"We can share custody," Marie begs. "Let me use it on weekends."

Terry laughs. "I can't believe you're fighting over a purse when you could choke the chicken."

Marie laughs in spite of herself. “Why would I want my own present, silly?”

“It's the funniest one here,” Terry opines.

“I have my secret Yankee Swap place,” she says smugly.

“Grandpa?” Jeffrey asks. “If you're not going to open your gift, can I?”

“Sure.” Jason hands him the round package the size of a cookie tin. He opens it.

It's... a sugar cookie tin. The ubiquitous kind.

“A *sewing kit?*” Jeffrey is clearly deflated. “Aw, man!” Prying the top off, Jeffrey halts. “Wait a minute. The top's not coming off. This is weird.” He patiently peels the clear plastic seal around the edge, then opens the tin.

Dumbfounded, he looks at Carol.

“Mom! There are cookies in this sewing kit!” He takes one that’s shaped like a pretzel, with big chunks of sugar on it, and pops the whole thing in his mouth, eyes wide. “Dis iff good.”

Meanwhile, the chicken lamp turns on, then off. On, then off. On and off in a steady rhythm that finally makes me turn to see my father, uh, choking the chicken, enthralled.

“What happened to your crazy gnome with the frog on a leash?” I ask Shannon.

“I hid it somewhere special at our place.”

“And...?”

She makes a face. “A place so special I can't find it! I had to ask Mom for a ThighMaster at the last minute.”

As we laugh, Dad looks at the box the chicken lamp came in, digging around, until he lifts a sheet of paper.

“What's this?”

13

Shannon

Mom instantly reddens and edges closer to him. "That's just a piece of packing paper. Nothing important."

Declan and Andrew share a look, while Terry watches Mom carefully before he says, "I know that logo."

"Logo?" James asks, squinting. "The light is so dim in here. I can't see anything."

"Because you need glasses, you vain old man," Pam says, scratching Spritzy's chin as she watches Mom trying to get the paper from James, who pivots and hands it to Declan.

My husband's face takes on an extraordinary look as he turns the paper around for everyone to see.

"*eBay?* Your secret store is *eBay?*" I gasp.

"I feel like my entire life is a lie!" Amy is aghast.

"Mom? Can I do the scratch tickets?" Jeffrey asks Carol. He holds a quarter in his hand, ready.

"Sure," she says absentmindedly. "They're yours."

Andrew and Declan crowd around him to watch just as a child's cry pierces the air upstairs. Amanda goes to see which kid it is as Jeffrey removes the silver film from the cards with the edge of the quarter, revealing numbers.

"We want three of the same kind," he explains.

"Like poker?" Andrew asks Declan. He shrugs.

"How the hell would I know?"

"*eBay?*" I hiss at Mom. "You told me it was Funicularelli's! Declan said you were lying to everyone."

"I wasn't lying!"

"You took me to a flea market, Marie. We could have gone to a good restaurant, had a nice lobster by the water, and done an eBay search on my phone," Declan says as Jeffrey continues to scratch.

"Two five hundreds!" he calls out excitedly, with one square left. "Come on, five hundred!"

Andrew leans in and whispers, "Is that a lot?"

"A thousand dollars is the most you can win," Carol explains.

Andrew rolls his eyes.

Jeffrey scratches the final square. Twenty dollars.

Moving on to the next ticket, his feverish scratching makes my skin itch, but I'm distracted by the sight of Amanda appearing with two sweaty little boys, Andrew moving fast to take Charlie out of her arms. Both toddlers cuddle immediately on their parents' shoulders.

Amy, Dad, and Carol are complaining bitterly to Mom, along with me.

"This one," I hear Jeffrey say, "has a top value of one thousand dollars."

"Half of James's gift," Dad interjects, obviously listening even as he referees his family's argument.

"I got two of them!" Jeffrey calls out.

Fingers interlace with mine as Declan pulls me a few feet away from everyone, pointing to the new snow falling in fat, lazy flakes. The backyard looks magical, and the soft Christmas music in the background makes the festive party even more homey.

A kiss on Christmas tastes like pine and family, like memories and futures, like a pause button held firm so the world doesn't spin quite as fast.

As our nephew scratches his way to a fantasy and my mother and sister do much the same, I realize I'm no different.

But I'm holding my dream in my arms.

And I wouldn't swap him for anything in the world.

:)

For years, I've hinted at Hamish (the McCormick family's Scottish football-playing cousin) and Amy having a love-hate flirtation with each other.

The hint is no more.

Shopping for a Turkey features Scottish football player Hamish McCormick and Amy Jacoby as they navigate unusual cultural norms, new traditions, and the undeniable attraction between these two characters who have been featured as minor players in Julia Kent's New York Times bestselling Shopping series.

It's their turn to pull the wishbone. ;)

Look for *Shopping for a Turkey*, coming in 2021.

ACKNOWLEDGMENTS

To Shelley Peters for her knowledge about scouting and patience in correcting my errors.

To Maria Connor, Elisa Reed, my husband Clark, and all of my beta readers – when you began reading this, you didn't know you'd take a logic test worthy of the LSAT or GREs! Figuring out who gave what and who received what in the Yankee Swap proved to be quite the challenge.

Any errors are solely mine.

OTHER BOOKS BY JULIA KENT

Shopping for a Billionaire: The Collection (Parts 1-5 in one bundle, 500 pages!)

- Shopping for a Billionaire 1
- Shopping for a Billionaire 2
- Shopping for a Billionaire 3
- Shopping for a Billionaire 4
- Christmas Shopping for a Billionaire

Shopping for a Billionaire's Fiancée
Shopping for a CEO
Shopping for a Billionaire's Wife
Shopping for a CEO's Fiancée
Shopping for an Heir
Shopping for a Billionaire's Honeymoon
Shopping for a CEO's Wife
Shopping for a Billionaire's Baby
Shopping for a CEO's Honeymoon
Shopping for a Baby's First Christmas
Shopping for a CEO's Baby
Shopping for a Yankee Swap

Little Miss Perfect
Fluffy
Perky

Feisty
Hasty

Her Billionaires
It's Complicated
Completely Complicated
It's Always Complicated

Random Acts of Crazy
Random Acts of Trust
Random Acts of Fantasy
Random Acts of Hope
Randomly Acts of Yes
Random Acts of Love
Random Acts of LA
Random Acts of Christmas
Random Acts of Vegas
Random Acts of New Year
Random Acts of Baby

Maliciously Obedient
Suspiciously Obedient
Deliciously Obedient
Christmasly Obedient

Our Options Have Changed (with Elisa Reed)
Thank You For Holding (with Elisa Reed)

ABOUT THE AUTHOR

New York Times and *USA Today* bestselling author Julia Kent writes romantic comedy with an edge. Since 2013, she has sold more than 2 million books, with 4 *New York Times* bestsellers and more than 19 appearances on the *USA Today* bestseller list. Her books have been translated into French and German, with more languages coming.

From billionaires to BBWs to new adult rock stars, Julia finds a sensual, goofy joy in every contemporary romance she writes. Unlike Shannon from Shopping for a Billionaire, she did not meet her husband after dropping her phone in a men's room toilet (and he isn't a billionaire).

She lives in New England with her husband and children in a household where everyone but Julia lacks the gene to change empty toilet paper rolls.

She loves to hear from her readers by email at jkentauthor@gmail.com, on Twitter @jkentauthor, on Facebook at https://www.facebook.com/jkentauthor . Visit her at http://jkentauthor.com

jkentauthor.com
julia@jkentauthor.com

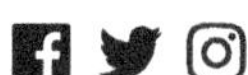